HANDBOOK OF KNOTS

HANDBOOK OF KNOTS

DES PAWSON

DK

DK
PUBLISHING,
INC.

London New York Munich
Melbourne Delhi

Senior Editor
Neil Lockley
Project Editor
Richard Gilbert
Project Designer
Jenisa Patel
Production Controller
Kevin Ward
DTP Designer
Adam Shepherd
DK India team
Ritu Malhotra, Pankaj Sharma,
Sunil Sharma, Sandeep Bhargava,
Aparna Sharma

Managing Editor
Adèle Hayward
Managing Art Editor
Karen Self
Category Publisher
Stephanie Jackson
Art Director
Peter Luff

First published in the United States
in 1998, this edition in 2004 by
DK Publishing, Inc.
375 Hudson Street
New York, New York 10014

A Penguin Company

2 4 6 8 10 9 7 5 3 7

Copyright © 1998, 2004
Dorling Kindersley Limited, London
Text copyright © 1998, 2004
Des Pawson

A Cataloging-in-Publication record
for this book is available from the
Library of Congress

ISBN 0 7566 0374 9

Reproduced by Colourscan,
Singapore
Printed in Hong Kong by Toppan

Discover more at
www.dk.com

CONTENTS

USING ROPE

STOPPER KNOTS

BINDING KNOTS

Bends

Hitches

Loops

Plaits & Sennits

Splices & Whippings

INTRODUCTION

K nots have been present at every stage of human progress, from their early use in making shelters and weapons to the sailor's dependence on knots in the great age of global exploration. During this time, thousands of knots have come into being for a vast range of tasks. The knots that I have chosen to include in this handbook are the most useful of those that are still known today, each one – whether centuries old or newly discovered – having proved to be reliable, safe, and effective when tied and used correctly.

TYING KNOTS SUCCESSFULLY

This book aims to help you identify the right knot for a task, and to tie it without getting into a frustrating tangle. Start by reading the section on Using Rope (p. 8) so that you understand the properties of different ropes, and how the condition and construction of a rope affects the use and effectiveness of a knot tied in it. Terms and techniques used in knot tying are also included in this section, and it is essential to familiarize yourself with these so that you can make the best use of the step-by-step instructions. If your attempts at tying a knot are repeatedly unsuccessful, check that the rope is positioned exactly as shown in the illustrations, and make sure the rope is placed under or over other parts of the knot as instructed. I also find it helpful to continually adjust the rope to retain the shape of the knot so that the parts described may be easily recognized. Happy knotting!

Jury Mast
Knot, p. 117

HOW TO USE THIS BOOK

To select a knot, first identify the knot family that is most appropriate for your task. The purposes of the different knot families are described at the start of each chapter. Use the icons and introductory text at the beginning of each knot to identify its categories of use and its properties. Refer to pp. 22–25 for knot-tying techniques common to many of the knots, and consult the Glossary (p. 171) for explanations of terms italicized in the text.

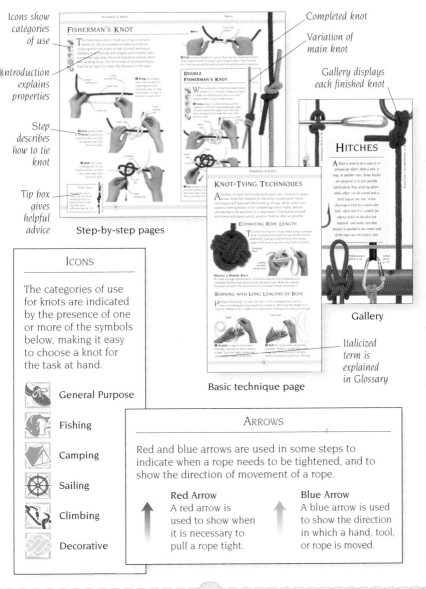

Icons show categories of use

Introduction explains properties

Step describes how to tie knot

Tip box gives helpful advice

Step-by-step pages

Completed knot

Variation of main knot

Gallery displays each finished knot

Gallery

Italicized term is explained in Glossary

Basic technique page

ICONS

The categories of use for knots are indicated by the presence of one or more of the symbols below, making it easy to choose a knot for the task at hand.

General Purpose

Fishing

Camping

Sailing

Climbing

Decorative

ARROWS

Red and blue arrows are used in some steps to indicate when a rope needs to be tightened, and to show the direction of movement of a rope.

Red Arrow
A red arrow is used to show when it is necessary to pull a rope tight.

Blue Arrow
A blue arrow is used to show the direction in which a hand, tool, or rope is moved.

Self-Stopped Coil, p. 19

Round Turn, p. 21

Fid, p. 21

Liquid Whipping, p. 16

Monofilament Polypropylene Rope, p. 12

Aramid Rope, p. 13

Marlingspike, p. 21

Swedish Fid, p. 21

Turn, p. 21

Manila Rope, p. 14

USING ROPE

U nderstanding the properties of rope and knowing how to keep it in good condition are essential to the effective application of knots. This chapter shows how to match a rope to a task according to its construction and the material from which it is made, and how to maintain and store rope so that it will remain safe to use. Basic terms, equipment, and techniques are introduced at the end of the chapter.

Palm, p. 21

Coil, p. 18

Sailor's Knife, p. 21

ROPE CONSTRUCTION

Rope is made of short fibers spun into yarn, which is made into flat or twisted strands. These strands are then twisted or braided to make the finished rope. This final stage of the construction of a rope, together with the material the rope is made from, will determine the texture, flexibility, stretch, and durability of the rope, as well as the way it handles when it is used to tie knots.

THREE-STRAND (LAID) ROPE

Three-strand, or laid, rope is made from yarns twisted together in one direction to make strands. Three strands are then twisted together in the opposite direction to form rope that is flexible and strong. It is the counteracting directions of the twists in the rope that give it strength and produce enough friction so that the rope holds its shape. Until World War Two all rope was of three-strand construction.

Three strands
are twisted
into rope

Strand is
made from
twisted yarn

Strand retains twist
when unlaid

Yarn is produced
from twisted fibers

Fibers

THE LAY OF THE ROPE

The direction of twist in three-strand rope is called the lay of the rope. Rope is described as S-laid (left-laid) or Z-laid (right-laid) according to whether the twist follows the line of the center part of the letter S or Z. Most three-strand rope is Z-laid. S-laid rope is usually found only in *cable*, made from three lengths of Z-laid rope twisted together.

S-Laid Rope

Z-Laid Rope

BRAIDED ROPE

The majority of modern rope is made by braiding yarns together. Braided rope is constructed in a variety of ways (below). The most common form is made up of a braided sheath of sixteen or more yarns covering an inner core of yarns, which may themselves be braided or lightly twisted together. The fibers of the braided sheath may provide the strength of the rope, or the sheath may serve to protect the load-bearing fibers of the inner core of the rope.

Hollow inner core is made from loosely braided strands

Strands are braided into seamless sheath

Yarns are lightly twisted into strands

Fibers are twisted into yarns

BRAIDED ROPE CONSTRUCTION

Braided rope with a sheath and a core is available in a number of different combinations of construction. Some braided ropes have no core at all. This variety gives a choice of ropes with a wide range of properties.

Strands are braided in pairs

Braided core *Sheath*

MULTIBRAIDED ROPE
This flexible rope does not kink. It is braided with two pairs of Z-laid and two pairs of S-laid strands (opposite).

BRAID ON BRAID
A braided core protected by a braided sheath gives a rope with less flexibility and stretch than a hollow braid (left).

Braided sheath has no core

Yarns are straight *Sheath*

HOLLOW BRAID
Found only in small sizes of rope, braided rope with no core is very flexible but tends to flatten during use.

PARALLEL CORE
This rope is very strong. Its braided cover protects a low-stretch core of parallel or lightly twisted yarns.

ROPE MATERIALS

T he properties of a rope are determined by the material from which it is made as well as its construction. A range of synthetic and natural materials is used in ropemaking, giving different ropes suitable for a variety of tasks. For the properties of rope materials in their different constructions, consult the chart on p. 15.

SYNTHETIC ROPE

S ince the invention of nylon in the 1930s, a number of types of synthetic fibers have been used to make ropes that are stronger, lighter, and more resistant to decay than natural ropes. They range in strength from all-purpose polypropylene ropes to the strongest ropes, made from aramid and materials such as Liquid Crystal Polymer (LCP) fibers. Synthetic rope is available in a variety of colors, allowing color-coding for different uses. It is more slippery than natural rope, and knots should be tested before use to make sure that they are secure.

Monofilament Polypropylene

Fibrillated Polypropylene

POLYPROPYLENE ROPE

Polypropylene fibers make low-cost, all-purpose ropes. They are light and float well, making them useful as rescue or short mooring lines. They have a low resistance to wear from abrasive surfaces and should be stored away from light, since they will disintegrate when exposed to ultraviolet light. Polypropylene ropes are available in a number of forms. Fibrillated fibers have the esthetic appeal of the natural rope, hemp (p. 14). Monofilament polypropylene rope is the most resistant to wear; multifilament fibers produce a softer rope that holds knots well; while rope made from split-film fibers is inexpensive. Staple-spun fibers produce a hairy rope which the hand can grip easily.

Multifilament Polypropylene

Split-Film Polypropylene

Staple-Spun Polypropylene

POLYESTER ROPE

Polyester rope, available as *three-strand* and *braided rope*, is nearly as strong as nylon rope (below) but retains more strength when wet and has a lesser degree of stretch. It is hard-wearing and does not float. Pre-stretched polyester rope, which gives minimum stretch during use, is also available.

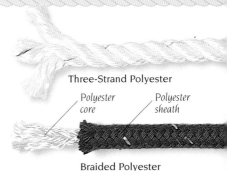

Three-Strand Polyester

Polyester core *Polyester sheath*

Braided Polyester

Nylon Monofilament Line

Three-Strand Nylon

Nylon sheath *Nylon core*

Braided Nylon

Nylon Multibraid

NYLON ROPE

Nylon was the first synthetic material to be used for ropemaking. It is still one of the strongest materials used to produce rope. Nylon rope has a lot of stretch, making it the most suitable rope for absorbing shock loads. It is often used to produce climbing ropes, which may need to absorb the energy of a climber's fall. When wet, nylon rope loses 5–25 percent of its strength. Like polyester rope (above), nylon rope is hard-wearing and does not float. It is available as three-strand, braided, and multibraid rope and is commonly used for fishing *line*.

NEW MATERIALS

Stronger rope-making materials, used as core inside a braided cover, are constantly being developed. Knots can greatly reduce their strength. Aramid has very low stretch, but does not work well over tight curves. Used in some fishing and kite lines, high-modulus polyethylene (HMP) is light and strong. Liquid crystal polymer (LCP) and poly [P-phenylene-3, 6-benzobisoxazole] (PBO) are new inventions. Quite expensive, all these materials are sold under various brand names.

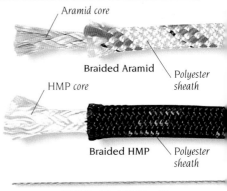

Aramid core

Braided Aramid

Polyester sheath

HMP *core*

Braided HMP

Polyester sheath

HMP Braided Fishing Line

13

NATURAL ROPE

Until the 20th century all rope was made from natural fibers, derived from a variety of plants. Usually made as *laid rope*, natural rope is esthetically pleasing but has a tendency to decay and become brittle. The following natural ropes are presented in order of strength, with the strongest appearing last.

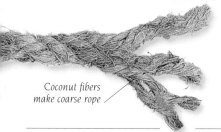

Coconut fibers make coarse rope

COIR

Coir rope is made from the fibers of coconut shells. It is the weakest of the natural ropes so it is made in large sizes to compensate. Coir rope floats and stretches. It is now rarely used except in India and the Pacific.

COTTON

Now used mainly as decorative rope, cotton was one of the most popular fibers used to make fishing nets, although it needed to be treated to prevent it from rotting. Cotton rope is stretchy and soft to the touch.

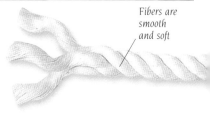

Fibers are smooth and soft

Rope is pale and hairy

SISAL

Sisal is a low-cost rope-making fiber produced from the leaves of the plant *Agave sisalana*. It can be purchased as a waterproofed rope for tasks and environments in which it will be exposed to moisture.

MANILA

Manila fibers derive from the leaves of the plant *Musa textilis*. High-quality manila rope, now rarely available, is as strong as hemp (below) and less susceptible to decay, It was widely used until World War Two.

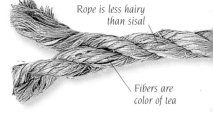

Rope is less hairy than sisal

Fibers are color of tea

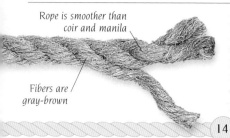

Rope is smoother than coir and manila

Fibers are gray-brown

HEMP

Hemp fibers, produced from the stalk of the plant *Cannabis sativa*, make the strongest of all natural ropes but have a tendency to decay. For centuries, hemp was the predominant rope-making fiber.

PROPERTIES OF ROPE MATERIALS

This chart is a general guide to the properties and main uses of ropes and lines made of different materials. It compares the relative strength of each type of rope or line, showing its minimum *breaking load* when new and when used in test conditions. Reduce these figures to 1/3 when using rope in conditions with no risk, to 1/6 for all-purpose usage, and to 1/10 in high-risk conditions. Always check that a rope is suitable for your purpose: rope that stretches will absorb shock; long mooring rope should not float; durable rope will be economical. Use the appropriate rope for splices and knots so that they hold well.

Material	Construction/Size	Breaking Load	Stretch	Floats	Durability	Spliceability	Knot-Holding	Main Uses
POLYPROPYLENE								
Fibrillated	three-strand (⁷⁄₁₆ in)	3,240 lb	medium	yes	fair	good	good	all/imitates hemp
Monofilament	three-strand (⁷⁄₁₆ in)	4,390 lb	medium	yes	fair	fair	fair	fishing
Multifilament	three-strand (⁷⁄₁₆ in)	4,390 lb	medium	yes	fair	good	good	low-cost mooring
Split-Film	three-strand (⁷⁄₁₆ in)	4,390 lb	medium	yes	poor	good	good	disposable
Staple-Spun	three-strand (⁷⁄₁₆ in)	4,390 lb	medium	yes	fair	good	good	low-cost mooring
POLYESTER	three-strand (⁷⁄₁₆ in)	4,920 lb	medium	no	good	fair	good	all
	braid on braid (⁷⁄₁₆ in)	5,290 lb	medium	no	good	poor	good	all
NYLON	three-strand (⁷⁄₁₆ in)	6,480 lb	medium/high	no	good	fair	good	climbing/mooring
	braided cover, twisted core (⁷⁄₁₆ in)	6,480 lb	medium	no	good	some	good	climbing
	multibraid (⁷⁄₁₆ in)	6,480 lb	medium/high	no	good	poor	good	mooring/anchoring
	monofilament fishing line (⁷⁄₁₆ in)	26 lb	none	no	good	-	good (fishing knots)	angling
ARAMID	braided core, polyester cover (⁷⁄₁₆ in)	14,330 lb	low	no	fair	very poor	poor	standing rigging
HMP	braided core, polyester cover (⁷⁄₁₆ in)	11,840 lb	low	yes	good	very poor	fair	running rigging
	braided fishing line (⁷⁄₁₆ in)	82 lb	none	no	good	some	fair	angling
COIR	three-strand (⁷⁄₁₆ in)	368 lb	very high	yes	poor	good	good	towing/mooring
COTTON	three-strand (⁷⁄₁₆ in)	1,300 lb	high	no	very poor	fair	good	decorative
SISAL	three-strand (⁷⁄₁₆ in)	2,060 lb	medium/high	no	very poor	good	good	all
MANILA	three-strand (⁷⁄₁₆ in)	2,310 lb	medium/high	no	poor	good	good	all
HEMP	three-strand (⁷⁄₁₆ in)	2,570 lb	medium/high	no	poor	good	good	all

ROPE MAINTENANCE

I t is important to maintain rope in good condition so that it can be relied on to perform effectively and safely. Caring for rope is also economical, since protecting it will help extend its useful life. Knots are most easily tied and will hold best in rope that is well looked after.

Use a scrubbing brush

CLEANING ROPE
Sand, grit, and oil will quickly wear out a rope from the inside. To prevent this, scrub dirty rope with a solution of liquid soap and warm water. Hang the rope to dry completely before coiling and storing it (p. 18).

BINDING ROPE ENDS

P revent a cut rope end from fraying with a permanent whipping (pp. 158–167), or with one of the temporary whippings given below. A cut end of synthetic rope can be sealed by melting it in a flame so that the fibers fuse together.

Liquid molds around end

Glue stiffens rope end

Plastic shrinks around rope

Tape is removable

LIQUID WHIPPING
Commercial liquid whippings are available. To seal the end of a rope, dip it into a liquid whipping and leave it to dry for a short period.

GLUE
Dip *thin line* or *small-diameter rope* into a latex-based or polyvinyl acetate glue, then leave it to dry. This will form an effective seal around the rope end.

PLASTIC TUBING
Plastic tubing is available to use as a whipping. Fit the tubing over the end of a rope, and hold it over hot steam so that it shrinks to form a tight seal.

ADHESIVE TAPE
Wind adhesive tape around a rope end. This will stiffen the end, helpful when tying some knots and when tucking strand ends for splicing (pp. 146–159).

PREVENTING CHAFE

Chafe, the result of repeatedly rubbing a section of rope against a surface, will cause a rope to wear out and become substantially weakened at that point. To prevent chafe, protect rope by covering either the rope or the surface. Never attempt to apply strain to a rope that is worn.

COVERING A ROPE
Plastic tubing can be used as effective protection for a rope that rubs against an abrasive surface. Slide a length of tight-fitting tubing that is longer than the affected area over a rope before using it.

Plastic tubing

Leather

COVERING A SURFACE
Rope can be protected from damage by minimizing the abrasiveness of surfaces against which it will rub. Attach a piece of smooth, hard-wearing material such as leather to a surface before allowing rope to come into contact with it. Sacking or canvas, inserted between a rope and a surface, can also be used to protect rope.

.USING A SHEEPSHANK

Strain can be taken off a worn area of a rope by tying it into a Sheepshank (p. 87). The worn area must form the center *turn* of the knot, leaving the tightened outer turns to take any strain.

Chafe

STORING ROPE

W hether uncoiling a new length of rope or storing an old rope, it is important to know how to uncoil and coil rope correctly to prevent it from tangling or acquiring a kink. Once a coil has been made, it must be secured to prevent it from unraveling.

UNCOILING AND COILING ROPE

A degree of twist is imparted to a rope whenever it is uncoiled or coiled. This can be reduced if the rope is uncoiled in the correct direction, and if the appropriate coiling method for the construction of the rope is used.

Z-laid rope

UNCOILING ROPE
Always uncoil Z-*laid rope* in a counterclockwise direction, whether from the outside or from the center of a coil. S-*laid rope* should always be uncoiled in a clockwise direction.

COILING THREE-STRAND ROPE
For Z-laid rope, make equal-sized circles of rope in a clockwise direction in the right hand, and transfer them as they are made to the left hand. Transfer circles of S-laid rope from one hand to the other in a counterclockwise direction.

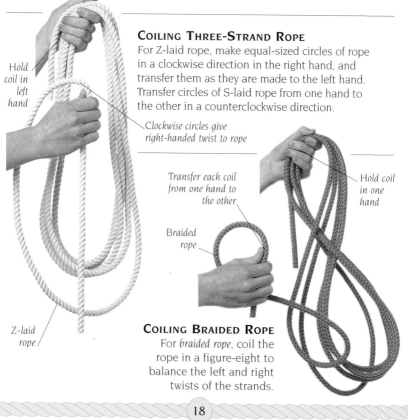

Hold coil in left hand

Clockwise circles give right-handed twist to rope

Transfer each coil from one hand to the other

Hold coil in one hand

Braided rope

Z-laid rope

COILING BRAIDED ROPE
For *braided rope*, coil the rope in a figure-eight to balance the left and right twists of the strands.

FINISHING COILS OF ROPE

A coil can be prevented from unraveling by binding it together with separate strands of rope or with the end of the rope. Some methods of binding a coil provide a *loop* that can be used to hang the coil up.

STOPPING A COIL

Use lengths of *thin line* or *small-diameter rope* to bind a large coil. With each length, tie a Constrictor Knot (p. 57) around the coil. Alternatively, tie a Packer's Knot (p. 54) or, for a quick binding, make two *turns* around the coil and tie a Square Knot (p. 48).

Constrictor Knot binds coil

SELF-STOPPED COIL

Loop

The most convenient method of preventing a coil from unraveling is to bind it with the end of the rope. The short end can be left loose, or a loop can be formed so that the coil can be hung up (below).

Loose end of rope

❶ **Coil** a length of rope, leaving the end of the rope free. Take the loose end of rope over the coil, then pull it through the center of the coil, leaving a small loop.

Turns hold end in place   *Loop*

❷ **Working** back from the loop, wrap the loose rope end around the coil to make three or more turns. Tuck the end through the loop. Slide the turns toward the loop to lock the loose end in place.

Coil

SELF-STOPPED COIL WITH A LOOP

To add a loop to a coil so that it can be hung up, first complete Step 1 of the Self-Stopped Coil (above). Double the remaining loose end back on itself to form a *bight*. Complete Step 2, making the turns with the bight, and passing the end of the bight through the initial loop to form the loop of the coil.

TERMS AND EQUIPMENT

Apart from a length of rope, the only requirement for tying the knots in this book is knowledge of the terms used to describe the different parts and configurations of rope. Most knots can be tied without equipment, although a few household and specialized items may be useful for tying and finishing off some knots.

TERMS

The terms in this section are only some of those developed over many centuries by tyers of knots. They identify which part of a rope is being used at a particular stage of tying a knot, and help distinguish between similar shapes made with a rope during the construction of a knot.

THE PARTS OF A ROPE

An end of a rope that is actively being used in the tying of a knot is known as a working end. The remaining, static part of the rope is known as the standing part.

Standing part
This is the part of a rope that is inactive during the tying of a knot.

Working end
This is the active part of a rope used while tying a knot.

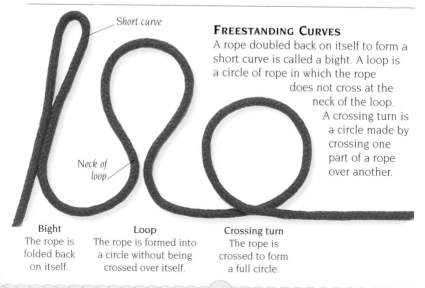

Short curve

FREESTANDING CURVES

A rope doubled back on itself to form a short curve is called a bight. A loop is a circle of rope in which the rope does not cross at the neck of the loop. A crossing turn is a circle made by crossing one part of a rope over another.

Neck of loop

Bight
The rope is folded back on itself.

Loop
The rope is formed into a circle without being crossed over itself.

Crossing turn
The rope is crossed to form a full circle.

TURNS AROUND AN OBJECT

A rope that completes one and a half circles around an object or another rope forms a round turn. A rope that passes around only one side of an object or rope forms a turn. (A series of circles is considered as multiple turns rather than round turns.)

Round turn
The rope forms one and a half circles around an object.

Turn
The rope is passed around one side of an object.

EQUIPMENT

E quipment for tying knots is available from a ship's chandler. Use a palm for protecting the hand when tying a whipping with a sailmaker's needle, a fid for separating stiff rope strands, and a Swedish fid for separating and tucking the strand ends of a splice (pp. 146–157). A marlingspike is helpful for untying tight knots. Use a sharp knife to trim rope, and temporarily prevent rope ends from fraying with adhesive tape (p. 16).

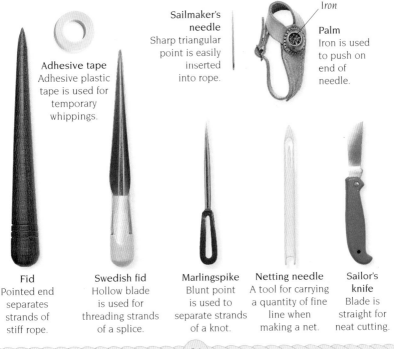

Sailmaker's needle
Sharp triangular point is easily inserted into rope.

Iron

Palm
Iron is used to push on end of needle.

Adhesive tape
Adhesive plastic tape is used for temporary whippings.

Fid
Pointed end separates strands of stiff rope.

Swedish fid
Hollow blade is used for threading strands of a splice.

Marlingspike
Blunt point is used to separate strands of a knot.

Netting needle
A tool for carrying a quantity of fine line when making a net.

Sailor's knife
Blade is straight for neat cutting.

KNOT-TYING TECHNIQUES

A number of basic knot-tying techniques are common to many knots, from the simplest to the most complicated. Some techniques will help with the handling of rope, while others are used in forming knots or for completing a knot neatly. Before attempting to tie any knot, it is important to familiarize yourself with these techniques, and to practice them as often as possible.

ESTIMATING ROPE LENGTH

To avoid running out of rope when tying a complex knot, estimate the length of rope needed before starting by making a dummy knot. If in doubt, begin with more rope than you think necessary.

Finished knot

Dummy resembles finished knot

MAKING A DUMMY KNOT

To make a rough dummy knot, follow the step-by-step instructions to complete the knot but leave out the detailed *tucks*. Mark the rope at the point at which the dummy knot is complete before releasing it.

WORKING WITH LONG LENGTHS OF ROPE

Pulling a long length of rope through a half-completed knot can be time-consuming and may result in confusion. Minimize the length of a rope by making it into a *bight* or bundle before tucking and pulling it through.

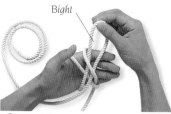

Bight

❶ **Double** a rope to be tucked through a strand so that it forms a *bight*. Tuck the bight under the appropriate strand of the knot.

Loose end

❷ **Pull** the loose end completely through. Triple or quadruple a very long rope to minimize its length before tucking and pulling it through.

UNLAYING AND LAYING ROPE

Some knots are made by separating (unlaying), then tying the individual strands of a *three-strand rope*. The strands may be twisted (laid) together again to complete the knot. Try to retain the original twist in each strand.

Unlay each strand a little at a time

UNLAYING ROPE
Carefully unwind two strands from the end of a three-strand rope. Tape the end of each strand (p. 16) to prevent it from fraying while a knot is being tied.

LAYING ROPE

❶ Twist the uppermost unlaid strand in the direction that it was originally laid. Position your thumb so that it finishes on top of the strand.

Thumb is on top of strand

Push strand with thumb

❷ Push the strand underneath the remaining two strands, and hold it in place. Twist and position each subsequent strand in this way until the required length of rope has been relaid.

FORMING A CROSSING TURN

Crossing turns are used as the basis of many knots. Twisting a rope between a finger and thumb is a quick method of forming a crossing turn, and helps prevent unwanted twist from developing in rope.

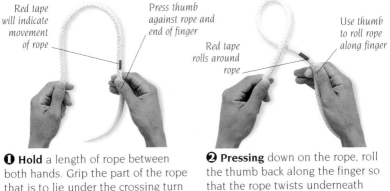

Red tape will indicate movement of rope

Press thumb against rope and end of finger

Red tape rolls around rope

Use thumb to roll rope along finger

❶ Hold a length of rope between both hands. Grip the part of the rope that is to lie under the crossing turn firmly between the finger and thumb.

❷ Pressing down on the rope, roll the thumb back along the finger so that the rope twists underneath itself to form a crossing turn.

WORKING A KNOT INTO SHAPE

O nce tied, many knots will need further tightening and adjusting to improve their appearance and effectiveness. Always ensure that the completed knot matches the image shown of the finished knot.

WORKING SLACK OUT

Rope is pulled loose

❶ To work slack out of a knot and to pull the strands evenly tight, pull on the rope at the start of the knot.

Rope is tightened little by little

Hand is turned to follow rope

❷ Working around the knot, pull on the rope again to tighten the part just loosened. Continue pulling the knot tight and even, working toward a loose end of rope.

Strand end

TIGHTENING STRAND ENDS

Tighten knots made with the *unlaid* strands of a *three-strand rope* by making several gentle pulls on each strand, one after the other. This will ensure that the strands are evenly tight.

WORKING STRANDS INTO PLACE

Use the fingers and thumb to push strands into position so that they lie snug and even. *Turns* can be twisted tight with the fingers and thumb.

Turns

ROLLING A SPLICE UNDERFOOT

The strands of spliced rope (pp.146–159) are tightened as a splice is being made. Improve the appearance of a splice after it has been completed by rolling it backward and forward underfoot so that the tucked strands are evenly distributed around the knot.

Spliced end

DOUBLING A KNOT

Threading an additional strand of rope alongside a knot will give it extra bulk and security, and can make some knots more decorative. If even more bulk is needed, thread the rope a third or fourth time through the knot.

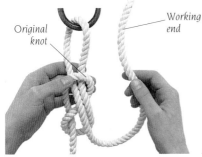

Original knot

Working end

Strands must not cross

❶ Using loose rope left at the start or the end of a knot (or, if instructed, using a second length of rope), thread the *working end* back into the start or finish of the knot.

❷ Making sure that the second strand of rope does not cross over the original strand, follow the path of the knot with the working end until all parts of the knot have been doubled.

FINISHING OFF A KNOT

The ends of a completed knot may need to be secured with a *seizing* to prevent the knot from coming undone. Secured loose ends should be trimmed to stop them from becoming tangled.

SEIZING ENDS
Bind a loose rope end to an adjacent strand of the knot with a seizing (p. 168).

Rope end

Cutting mat

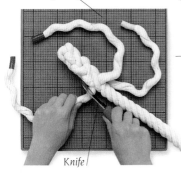

Rope end

Knife

TRIMMING ENDS
Use a sharp knife (p. 21) to trim the ends of a knot. The ends of a whipping can be trimmed close to the rope. Leave a short stump of rope on other knots so that the ends do not work loose when strain is applied to the knot.

Matthew Walker Knot, p. 38

Double Overhand Knot, p. 29

Sink Stopper, p. 32

Monkey's Fist, p. 34

Crown Knot, p. 36

Stopper Knot, p. 31

Slipped Figure-Eight, p. 30

Slipped Overhand Knot, p. 28

Manrope Knot, p. 40

STOPPER KNOTS

Stopper knots are used to bind the strands at the end of a rope so that they do not fray, to stop a rope from slipping through a hole, to weight a rope, or to provide a handhold. They are usually tied at the end of a rope, although some can be tied within the length of a rope. This family of knots includes some of the simplest and most commonly used knots.

OVERHAND KNOT

The simplest of all knots, the Overhand Knot has been in use for as long as there has been material that can be knotted. Useful as a handhold as well as a stopper, it is tied at regular intervals along lifelines to prevent the rope from slipping through the hands. It also forms the basis of many other knots, particularly in the loop, bend, and hitch families. Once tied and put under strain, it is very difficult to untie.

Crossing turn

Working end

❶ Make a *crossing turn* by taking the *working end* of a rope behind the *standing part*.

Standing part

SLIPPED OVERHAND KNOT

Tucking a *bight* through a *crossing turn* produces a useful stopper knot that can be untied as easily as it can be tied. Allow a long *working end* for forming the bight. This knot can be tied at the end or in the middle of a rope.

❶ Complete Step 1 as for the Overhand Knot (above). Double the *working end* to form a *bight*, then pass the bight through the *crossing turn*.

Crossing turn

Pass bight through turn from front to back

Crossing turn tightens around bight

Standing part

Bight

❷ To complete the knot, pull on the bight and on the *standing part*. A tug on the short working end will release the knot.

Short working end

2 Bring the working end to the front of the knot, then pass it through the crossing turn.

Working end

Crossing turn

Standing part

Working end

3 Pull on the working end and on the standing part to tighten the knot.

DOUBLE OVERHAND KNOT

The Double Overhand Knot is bulkier than the Overhand Knot (opposite). If required, this knot can be made even larger with additional *turns* made around the *crossing turn*. Knots with many turns are known as *blood knots*, since they were used on the lashes of a cat-o'-nine tails.

Crossing turn

First turn

Second turn

1 Complete Steps 1–2 as for the Overhand Knot. Tuck the *working end* a second time through the *crossing turn*.

First turn

2 Pull tight on both ends of the rope. Push the first *turn* into the center of the knot.

29

FIGURE-EIGHT KNOT

An extra *turn* made to the Overhand Knot (p. 28) results in the Figure-Eight, which has more bulk. It is also an easier knot to untie, particularly if the knot has been put under great strain. It can be quickly tied and is commonly used by sailors to prevent a rope from slipping through a hole.

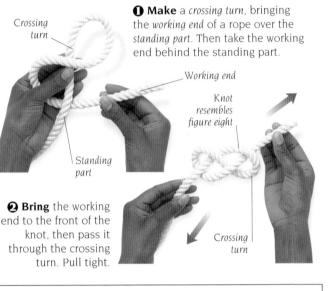

❶ **Make** a *crossing turn*, bringing the *working end* of a rope over the *standing part*. Then take the working end behind the standing part.

Crossing turn

Working end

Knot resembles figure eight

Standing part

❷ **Bring** the working end to the front of the knot, then pass it through the crossing turn. Pull tight.

Crossing turn

SLIPPED FIGURE-EIGHT

Where a stopper knot may need to be untied quickly, use a Slipped Figure-Eight, which can be released with a tug on the *working end*.

Bight

❶ Complete Step 1 of the Figure-Eight (above). Form a *bight* with the *working end*, and tuck it through the *crossing turn*. Pull the knot tight.

Working end

STOPPER KNOT

Although it is tied in a different manner, the Stopper Knot is a variation of the Double Overhand Knot (p. 29). It is among the most decorative of stopper knots. The finished knot is large enough to add weight to the end of a rope that needs to be thrown.

Working end

❶ Leaving a long *working end*, hold a rope in one hand. Take the working end over the rope to make a *round turn* around two fingers.

Round turn

Turns anchor rope

❷ Continue to make a series of at least five *turns* around the fingers and over the *standing part*.

Standing part

Working end

Thumb acts as guide

❸ Remove the knot from the fingers, and slip it over a thumb. Tuck the working end inside the turns, then pull it through.

Turns tighten around rope

❹ Pull the knot tight. Work it into shape (p. 24) so that the turns lie neatly side by side on the finished knot.

SINK STOPPER

This substantial knot is particularly useful for preventing a thin rope from slipping out of a large hole. The knot needs to be carefully tightened (p. 24) so that it keeps its shape.

❶ Make a *crossing turn* by taking the *standing part* behind the *working end*. Make a *bight* by doubling back the standing part, then pass it through the crossing turn from front to back.

Bight

Crossing turn

Working end

Standing part

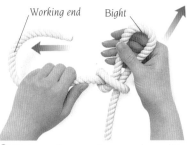

Working end   *Bight*

❷ Tighten the crossing turn by pulling on the bight and the working end. The turn may need to be pushed downward to work the *body* of the knot into shape.

Crossing turn

Body of knot

Working end

❸ Bring the working end across the body of the knot, laying it parallel to the tightened turn.

❹ Keeping the rope parallel to the crossing turn, take the working end around to the back of the knot. Pass it through the bight and pull through.

Working end   *Bight*

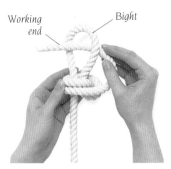

Bight

Working end

Standing part

❺ Hold the body of the knot in one hand, then pull on the standing part to tighten the bight over the working end. Work the knot into shape.

STEVEDORE KNOT

The Stevedore Knot is developed from the start of the Figure-Eight Knot (p. 30), with two *turns* added to form a bigger, bulkier knot that can still be easily untied. The name of the knot is derived from its use by stevedores (dock workers) as a stopper knot.

Crossing turn

❶ Bring a long *working end* over the *standing part* of a rope to form a *crossing turn*. Pass the working end behind and then in front of the standing part below the crossing turn.

Working end

Standing part

Keep eye of turn open

Crossing turn

Working end

❷ Pass the working end behind the standing part one more time to form the final *turn* around the rope, then bring the working end to the front of the knot.

Standing part

❸ Insert the working end through the crossing turn, passing it from the front to the back of the knot.

Working end

❹ Tighten the knot by pulling on the standing part and working end. The knot can be tightened still further by pulling the two additional turns against the standing part.

Standing part

Turns

MONKEY'S FIST

This is the most suitable knot to tie if a weight is needed at the throwing end of a *heaving line*, since a heavy object can be inserted into its center. To achieve a knot that is decorative as well as useful, make sure that all *turns* are even and, when working the knot into shape (p. 24), tighten the strands around the weight a little at a time. The Monkey's Fist can be painted if it will be used as a permanent fixture.

First cycle of turns

❶ **Estimate** (p. 22) the amount of rope needed at the end of a rope to complete the knot. Working toward the end of the rope, make a cycle of three *turns* around one hand.

First turn of second cycle

Rope holds first turn in place

Rope changes direction

❷ **Turn** the rope at a right angle across the completed turns. Make a second cycle of three turns across the first, making sure that the rope holds the first turn in place where it changes direction.

First cycle of turns

Third turn

Second cycle of turns

❸ **Tuck** the rope through the first cycle of turns beside the second. Pull the length of the rope through to tighten the third turn of the second cycle.

④ Take the rope over the second cycle of turns, and tuck it back through the first cycle. Pull the rope through.

Second cycle of turns

Second cycle of turns

First cycle of turns

⑤ Make three turns around the second cycle, tucking them through the first cycle of turns as Steps 3–4. Lay the three turns over the rope where it changes direction as before in order to anchor the rope in place.

Wooden ball weights knot

Rope exits knot

⑥ Insert a round weight – a wooden ball is ideal – into the center of the knot. It is easiest to insert the weight into the gap where the rope and rope end exit the knot.

Tuck trimmed rope end into knot for a neat finish

⑦ Trim (p. 25) the end of the rope, then tuck it between the knot and the weight. Work the knot into shape around the weight, pulling the strands of each cycle tight.

CROWN KNOT

Crown Knot: overview

The Crown Knot is used as a basis for more complex knots. Made with the strand ends of *three-strand rope*, the downward *tucks* are made in a counterclockwise direction for *Z-laid rope*.

Crown Knot: side view

❶ Unlay (p. 23) the strands at the end of a rope, leaving long strand ends. Pick up a first strand end, and lay it over the second strand end, allowing a *bight* to remain between the two.

Second strand end

First strand end

Bight

First strand end

Second strand end

Third strand end

❷ Pass the second strand end over the first and third strand ends.

Bight

Second strand end

❸ Pick up the third strand end, take it over the second, then tuck it down through the bight left by the first strand end.

Third strand end

Strand ends fall downward from knot

Interlocking triangle

❹ Tighten the knot by pulling gently on the three strand ends so that they form an interlocking triangle.

WALL KNOT

The Wall Knot is tied in a similar way to the Crown Knot (opposite) and is also used as the basis for other knots. Whip (pp. 160-167) the ends before using it as a stopper knot. To tie the Wall Knot, each strand end is passed around and underneath the next strand end.

Wall Knot: overview

❶ Unlay (p. 23) the strands at the end of a rope, leaving long strand ends. Take a first strand end, and pass it under the second strand end in a counterclockwise direction. Leave a *bight* between the two strand ends.

First strand end

Second strand end

Bight

First strand end

Second strand end

Third strand end

❷ Take the second strand end around and under the first strand end, then take it under the third strand end.

Third strand end

Bight

❸ Bring the third strand end under the second. Tuck it up through the bight formed with the first strand end.

Strand ends rise upward from knot

Second strand end

❹ Gently tighten all three strand ends to work the Wall Knot into shape (p. 24).

Wall Knot: side view

MATTHEW WALKER KNOT

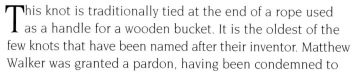

This knot is traditionally tied at the end of a rope used as a handle for a wooden bucket. It is the oldest of the few knots that have been named after their inventor. Matthew Walker was granted a pardon, having been condemned to death as a criminal, when he tied the knot in the middle of a length of rope and the judge could neither tie nor untie it.

Eye of bight

Bight

Bight

❶ Tie a loose Wall Knot (p. 37), leaving long strand ends. Ensure that there is a large *eye* in of each of the three *bights* formed by the Wall Knot.

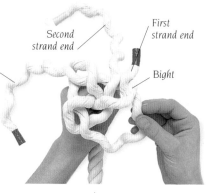

Second strand end

First strand end

Third strand end

Bight

❷ Choose a first strand end, take it around the Wall Knot in a counterclockwise direction, then tuck it up through the bight from which the next strand end exits.

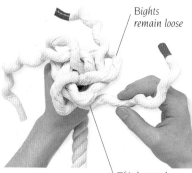

Bights remain loose

❸ Repeat with the second and third strand ends. Pull all the strand ends through, working each one a little at a time to keep the knot even.

Third strand end tucks up along first

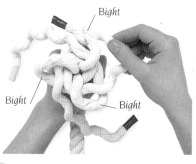

Bight

Bight

Bight

❹ Continuing to work in a counterclockwise direction, make a second cycle of *tucks*, passing each strand end through the next bight from which a strand end exits.

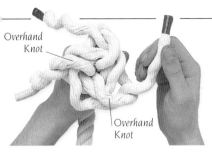

Overhand Knot

Overhand Knot

❺ Pull the strand ends gently through so that the bights remain even. Note that the knot is made up of a series of interlocking Overhand Knots (p. 28).

❻ Draw up the knot over the part of the rope that remains *laid*, pulling on each strand end in turn.

Laid rope

Pull strand ends tight little by little

Knot lies at junction of laid and unlaid strands

❼ Work the knot into shape (p. 24), tightening the strands so that they bed neatly side by side. If the knot is at the end of a rope, trim (p. 25) the strand ends.

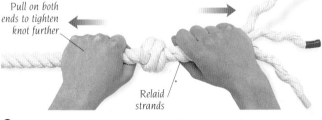

Pull on both ends to tighten knot further

Relaid strands

❽ If the knot is within the length of the rope, relay (p. 23) the loose strand ends. From time to time, twist the strands together in the direction that they have been relaid.

MANROPE KNOT

This is the traditional knot made for decorating the ends of handrail ropes used when boarding ships. For added effect, strands may be covered with canvas before being tied, and the whole knot painted in different colors. The Manrope Knot is made up of a Crown Knot (p. 36) tied on top of a Wall Knot (p. 37). When these knots are doubled, make sure that each strand is positioned on the same side as previous strands. Tighten the knot little by little.

❶ Tie a loose Wall Knot with long strand ends, working in a counterclockwise direction.

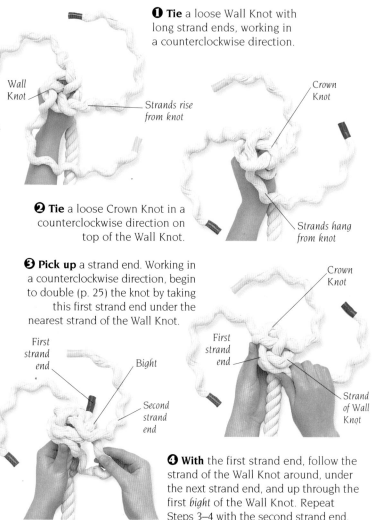

Wall Knot

Strands rise from knot

Crown Knot

❷ Tie a loose Crown Knot in a counterclockwise direction on top of the Wall Knot.

Strands hang from knot

❸ Pick up a strand end. Working in a counterclockwise direction, begin to double (p. 25) the knot by taking this first strand end under the nearest strand of the Wall Knot.

First strand end

Bight

Second strand end

Crown Knot

First strand end

Strand of Wall Knot

❹ With the first strand end, follow the strand of the Wall Knot around, under the next strand end, and up through the first *bight* of the Wall Knot. Repeat Steps 3–4 with the second strand end.

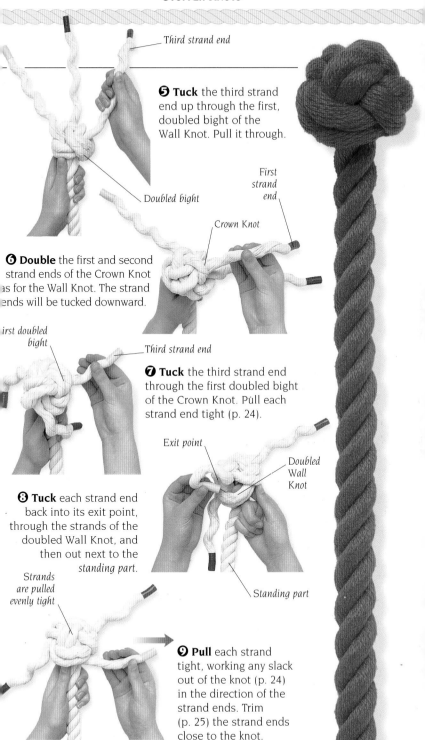

Third strand end

❺ Tuck the third strand end up through the first, doubled bight of the Wall Knot. Pull it through.

First strand end

Doubled bight

Crown Knot

❻ Double the first and second strand ends of the Crown Knot as for the Wall Knot. The strand ends will be tucked downward.

First doubled bight

Third strand end

❼ Tuck the third strand end through the first doubled bight of the Crown Knot. Pull each strand end tight (p. 24).

Exit point

Doubled Wall Knot

❽ Tuck each strand end back into its exit point, through the strands of the doubled Wall Knot, and then out next to the standing part.

Strands are pulled evenly tight

Standing part

❾ Pull each strand tight, working any slack out of the knot (p. 24) in the direction of the strand ends. Trim (p. 25) the strand ends close to the knot.

Diamond Knot

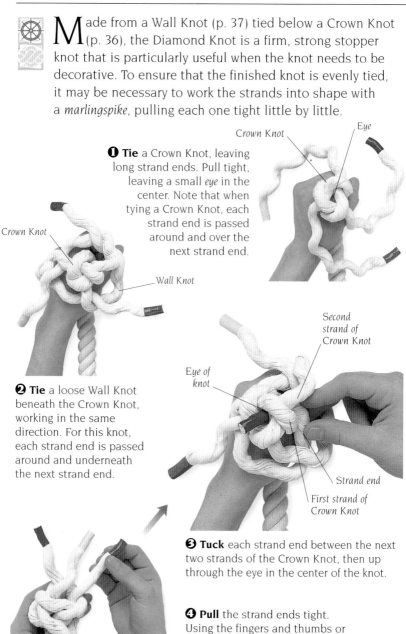

Made from a Wall Knot (p. 37) tied below a Crown Knot (p. 36), the Diamond Knot is a firm, strong stopper knot that is particularly useful when the knot needs to be decorative. To ensure that the finished knot is evenly tied, it may be necessary to work the strands into shape with a *marlingspike*, pulling each one tight little by little.

❶ Tie a Crown Knot, leaving long strand ends. Pull tight, leaving a small *eye* in the center. Note that when tying a Crown Knot, each strand end is passed around and over the next strand end.

Crown Knot

Eye

Crown Knot

Wall Knot

❷ Tie a loose Wall Knot beneath the Crown Knot, working in the same direction. For this knot, each strand end is passed around and underneath the next strand end.

Second strand of Crown Knot

Eye of knot

Strand end

First strand of Crown Knot

❸ Tuck each strand end between the next two strands of the Crown Knot, then up through the eye in the center of the knot.

❹ Pull the strand ends tight. Using the fingers and thumbs or a marlingspike, work the knot into shape (p. 24), forming a neat braid around the *laid* part of the rope.

Laid rope

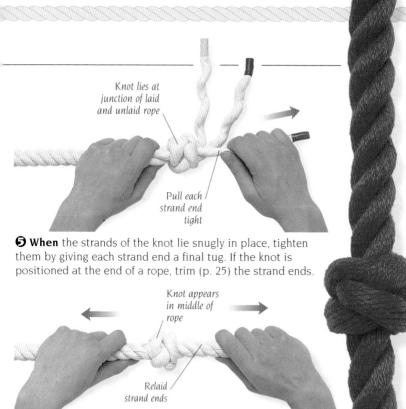

Knot lies at
junction of laid
and unlaid rope

Pull each
strand end
tight

❺ When the strands of the knot lie snugly in place, tighten
them by giving each strand end a final tug. If the knot is
positioned at the end of a rope, trim (p. 25) the strand ends.

Knot appears
in middle of
rope

Relaid
strand ends

❻ If the knot is positioned within the length of the rope, relay
(p. 23) the strand ends, twisting the rope at intervals in the
direction of the *lay* of the rope. To tighten the knot still further,
give the rope a tug on both ends from time to time.

DOUBLE DIAMOND KNOT

Double (p. 25) the Diamond
Knot to produce a larger,
more handsome knot. Tie a
Crown Knot and a Wall Knot as
for Steps 1–2 of the Diamond
Knot (opposite). Double the
Crown Knot, then double the
Wall Knot. Bring the strand ends
up through the *eye* in the center
of the knot. Tighten the Double
Diamond Knot and relay the
strands by following Steps 4–6
of the Diamond Knot.

Granny Knot, p. 49

True Lover's Knot, p. 47

Constrictor Knot, p. 57

Sailor's Cross, p. 47

Turk's Head – Four-Lead Five-Bight, p. 62

Clove
Hitch, p. 56

BINDING
KNOTS

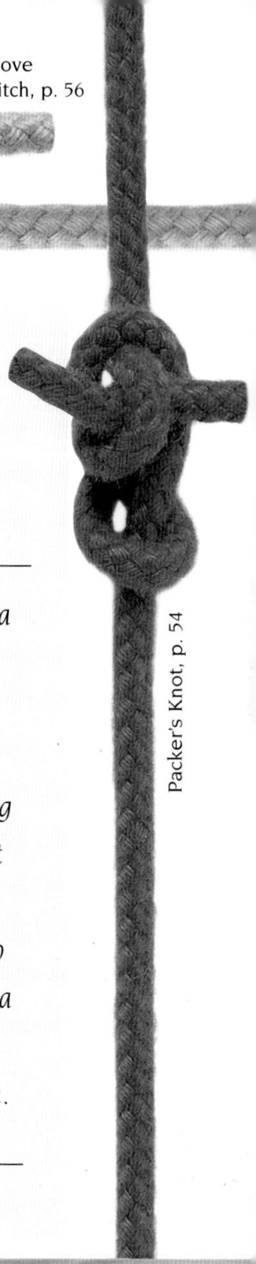

Packer's Knot, p. 54

Square Knot, p. 48

A *binding knot is used to secure a
length of rope passed around an
object. Often used for tying up
parcels, from bundles of logs to
gift-wrapped presents, most binding
knots can be pulled tight and kept
fixed in place. Avoid using a
binding knot as a bend to join two
lengths of rope, or as a hitch to tie a
rope to an object, since the knot is
likely to come undone under strain.*

Boa
Knot,
p. 59

Surgeon's Knot, p. 51

Slipped Square Knot, p. 49

Thief Knot, p. 50

Timber Hitch, p. 58

Turquoise Turtle, p. 52

Turk's Head – Five-Lead Four-Bight, p. 64

Turk's Head – Three-Lead Four-Bight, p. 60

TRUE LOVER'S KNOT

This is one of many knots used as a symbol of the binding love between two people. It is made up of two separate Overhand Knots (p. 28) interlinked and bound tightly together, each one a mirror of the other.

❶ **Tie** an Overhand Knot within a length of rope. Pass the *working end* of a second rope up through the Overhand Knot, then lay it over its own *standing part* to form a *crossing turn*.

Overhand Knot

Standing part

Crossing turn

Working end

❷ **Tuck** the working end of the second rope through this crossing turn to tie a second Overhand Knot.

Second Overhand Knot

Working end

❸ **Pull** on the ends of both Overhand Knots to tighten the knot.

Knots are bound tightly

SAILOR'S CROSS

This simple cross is tied with the two ends of a single length of rope. To start, follow Steps 1–2 of the True Lover's Knot (above) to link two loose Overhand Knots.

❶ Pull the center strands of each knot through the crossed strands of the opposite knot. Pull on the upper *loop* to form a cross.

Upper loop

Centre strands

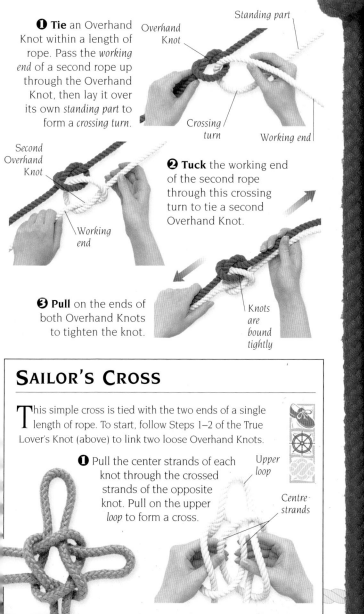

SQUARE KNOT

A very simple binding knot, the Square Knot was traditionally used to tie up a reef (sail) – so it is often called a Reef Knot. It is one of a small number of knots that most people know of, but it is often tied and used incorrectly. Avoid tying a Granny Knot (opposite) by making sure that the two *tucks* are made in opposite directions, and use the Square Knot only as a binding knot; it must not be used to join two lengths of rope, since it can easily come undone.

Right working end

Left working end

❶ Take the left *working end*, and cross it over the right working end.

Left working end tucks through right working end

Right working end tucks through left working end

Left working end

❷ Tuck the left working end under the right working end.

❸ Tuck the working end that now lies on the right side of the knot over and under the working end on the left side of the knot.

Working ends lie on same side of knot

Finished knot is square

❹ Pull on the right and left working ends to tighten the knot.

SLIPPED SQUARE KNOT

The Slipped Square Knot can be quickly untied by tugging on the short end of the *bight*. Start with a long *working end* in the left hand so that there is enough rope to make into a bight.

Left working end

Bight

❶ **Complete** Steps 1–2 of the Square Knot (opposite). Form a *bight* with the *working end* lying on the right side of the knot.

Left working end

Bight

❷ **Tuck** the bight over and under the left working end. Pull on the left working end and on the bight to tighten the knot around the bight.

GRANNY KNOT

The Granny Knot is an incorrectly tied Square Knot (opposite), and does not have the same square form. Each *tuck* of one *working end* over the other is made from the same rather than from the opposite side of the knot.

THIEF KNOT

Similar in appearance to a Square Knot (p. 48), this knot was once used to detect thieves. After untying what seemed to be a Square Knot tied around a sack or bag, a thief would then carefully retie a Square Knot. But the short ends of the Thief Knot lie on opposite sides of the knot, not on the same side – clear evidence of unwelcome interference.

Working end

❶ Pass a length of rope around the item to be bound. Fold one end of the rope back on itself to form a *loop*. Bring the *working end* up through the loop, then take it underneath the neck of the loop.

Neck of loop

Loop

Working end

Loop

❷ Tuck the working end back down through the loop.

Hold neck of loop in place

❸ Pull on the working end and on the short end of the loop to tighten the knot. Note that the ends lie on either side of the knot.

Short end of loop

Working end

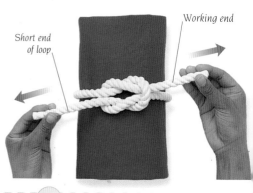

SURGEON'S KNOT

Another variation of the Square Knot (p. 48), this knot is used by surgeons to tie off the ends of blood vessels. The extra *tuck* adds enough friction to keep the knot in place until it is completed. A further tuck will make the knot even more secure.

Right working end

Left working end

❶ Take a length of rope around an item. Tuck the *working end* on the left twice around the working end on the right.

Right working end

❷ Tuck the working end on the right over then under the working end on the left.

Left working end

Working end

❸ Pull on both working ends to tighten the knot. Trim (p. 25) the working ends if required.

SURGEON'S KNOT WITH SECOND TUCK

Second tuck

To make sure that a slippery rope does not work loose, tuck the right *working end* twice around the working end on the left at Step 2 of the Surgeon's Knot (above). Pull tight.

TURQUOISE TURTLE

Named after the boutique where it was discovered, the Turquoise Turtle contains elements of the Square Knot (p. 48) and the Surgeon's Knot (p. 51). It is the perfect knot for tying shoelaces (since it almost never comes undone), it looks neat, and it can be tied very quickly. To complete this knot successfully, make sure that the loose ends are positioned on the inside of the knot exactly as shown.

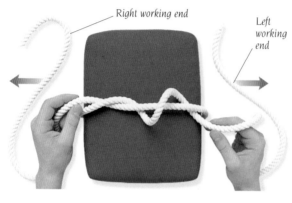

Right working end

Left working end

❶ Using a long length of rope to bind an item, tuck the left *working end* of the rope twice under the right working end. Pull both ends tight.

❷ Double each working end back on itself to form two large *bights* of equal size, folding the rope so that the loose ends are positioned on the insides of the bights. Place the right bight on top of the left bight.

Right bight

Left bight

Loose end

Loose end

Right bight

Loose end

Left bight

Loose end

❸ Tuck the right bight under the left bight, and pull through. Make sure that the loose ends remain on the inside of the knot.

Single strand

Bundle of bight and loose end

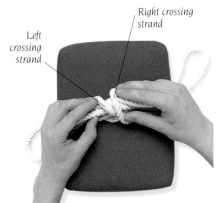

❹ Hold the bight and the loose end now on the right of the knot in a bundle. Tuck this bundle through the single strand that remains on the right. Gently tighten the knot by pulling on the two bights (not on the loose ends).

Right crossing strand

Left crossing strand

❺ Push the two crossing strands that have formed in the center of the knot toward each other, then cross the right strand over the left strand. These strands will help to keep the knot in place.

Crossing strands

Loose end

❻ To tighten the knot, pull on both bights, leaving the loose ends free. Push the crossing strands back into place if they work loose.

Bight

PACKER'S KNOT

Essentially a Figure-Eight Knot (p. 30) tied around the *standing part* of a rope, the Packer's Knot allows a binding to be tightened after the knot is tied. A finishing *half-hitch* is tied to lock the knot in place. This is the knot that butchers use to tie up joints of meat.

Parcel

❶ Pass the *working end* of a rope over then under the parcel to be bound. Bring it back up into the center of the parcel. Pass it over then under the *standing part*.

Working end
Standing part

Standing part

Crossing turn

❷ Form a *crossing turn* around the standing part by laying the working end over itself. Then tuck it underneath itself.

Standing part

Working end

Eye

❸ Tuck the working end down through the crossing turn, making sure that it passes first over the standing part. This forms the Figure-Eight.

Figure-Eight

❹ Pull on the loose standing part against the Figure-Eight to tighten the binding around the parcel.

Loose standing part

Figure-Eight

Half-hitch

❺ Secure the knot with a finishing half-hitch by passing the loose standing part around the short working end, then tucking the loose standing part under itself. The half-hitch can also be twisted into place with the fingers and thumb (p. 23).

Short working end

Loose standing part

❻ Pull on the loose standing part against the working end to tighten the half-hitch and lock the binding in place. Trim (p. 25) the ends of the rope.

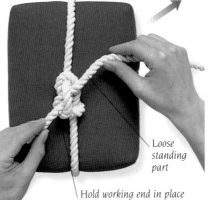

Loose standing part

Hold working end in place

CLOVE HITCH

Made up of two *half-hitches*, the Clove Hitch is one of the most commonly tied binding knots. It can be used in a number of ways and forms the basis of many other knots. In addition to functioning as a binding knot, the Clove Hitch can be tied around stakes to rope off an area. If used as a mooring knot it should be used only temporarily, leaving a long loose end, or tying a half-hitch around the *standing part* for more security.

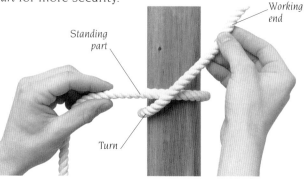

Standing part

Working end

❶ Pass a length of rope around a pole to form a *turn*, crossing the *working end* of the rope over its *standing part*.

Turn

CLOVE HITCH – SECOND METHOD

A quick method of tying a Clove Hitch can be used if the rope is not under strain while the knot is being tied. This method allows the hitch to be passed over the end of a pole, or to be clipped on to a *screwgate karabiner*.

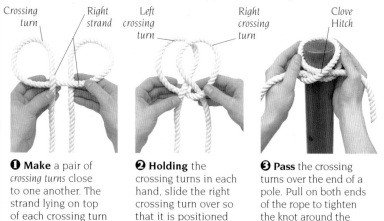

Crossing turn

Right strand

Left crossing turn

Right crossing turn

Clove Hitch

❶ Make a pair of *crossing turns* close to one another. The strand lying on top of each crossing turn should be the right strand of each turn.

❷ Holding the crossing turns in each hand, slide the right crossing turn over so that it is positioned on top of the left crossing turn.

❸ Pass the crossing turns over the end of a pole. Pull on both ends of the rope to tighten the knot around the pole. Work the Clove Hitch into shape (p. 24).

Second
turn

First
turn

Working
end

❷ Take the working end around the pole once again, making a second turn in the same direction as the first.

❸ Keeping the rope parallel to the first turn, tuck the working end underneath the second turn. Pull on the working end and on the standing part to tighten the knot.

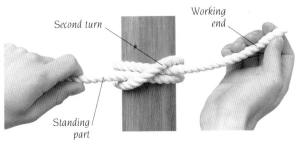

Second turn

Working
end

Standing
part

CONSTRICTOR KNOT

The Constrictor Knot deserves to be widely known since, tied around almost anything, it will form a tighter binding than the Clove Hitch (above). The final *tuck* of this knot holds the rope in place as the ends are pulled tight. If strain has been put on the rope, it may have to be cut rather than untied. The Constrictor Knot is most effective when tied in *thin line*.

❶ Repeat Steps 1–3 of the Clove Hitch. Before pulling the knot tight, pass the *working end* over, then under the first *turn*. Pull the working end through. Pull tight as for Step 3 of the Clove Hitch.

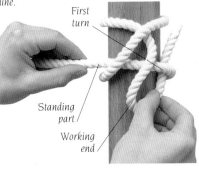

First
turn

Standing
part

Working
end

TIMBER HITCH

The more strain that is put on the Timber Hitch the tighter it grips, yet it is easy to untie. Traditionally it has been used for tying a length of rope around a pole or a bundle of logs.

Working end

Standing part

❶ Pass the end of a length of rope around a pole, leaving a long *working end* on one side. Take the working end over the pole and around the *standing part*.

❷ Cross the working end over itself, then tuck it underneath itself, working back around the pole.

Working end

Working end

Working end

❸ Continue tucking the working end around itself until a series of *tucks* has been formed around the pole.

Tuck

PULLING A POLE

If the pole or log bundle will be dragged through water or across land, an extra *half-hitch* can be added at the near end of the pole. The half-hitch acts as a stabilizer, preventing the pole from swinging around while it is being moved.

Working end is jammed against pole

❹ Pull hard on the standing part against the knot to tighten it. Maintain this tension on the rope to keep the Timber Hitch in place.

BOA KNOT

The Boa Knot, slipped over the end of a pole, is simple and ingenious. It can be used instead of the Constrictor Knot (p. 57) if a decorative as well as practical knot is required.

Half turn

❶ Coil (p. 18) a rope between two hands, making two and a half *turns*. Each turn should be at least twice the diameter of the pole around which the knot will be tied.

❷ **Holding** the coil in each hand, twist one hand toward you and the other hand away to form two loops in the coil.

Loop

Loop

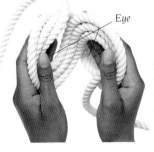

Eye

❸ **Fold** the two loops together, making sure that the *eye* in the center of each loop remains open.

Crossed strands

❹ **Slide** the folded loops over the end of the pole, keeping the crossed strands at the front of the knot.

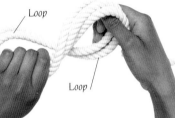

Crossed loops hold knot in place

❺ **Work** the loops into shape (p. 24), pulling on the strands little by little to tighten them against the pole. Pull on both ends to tighten the knot.

TURK'S HEAD – THREE-LEAD FOUR-BIGHT

The knots known as Turk's Heads are essentially continuous *braids*. *Lead* refers to the number of strands in the braid, and *bight* to the number of curved sides of the finished knot. These decorative knots are usually tied around a pole or hand, but can be flattened to make a small mat.

❶ Estimate (p. 22) the length of rope needed for the knot. Make a *turn* around the palm of one hand, passing the *working end* first over the top of the hand. Cross the working end over the *standing part* from right to left.

Working end
First turn

Standing part

❷ Make a second turn around the hand to the left of the first. Cross the working end over the turn from left to right.

First turn

Working end

Working end   Second turn

Working end

First turn

❸ Tuck the working end through the first turn at the top of the hand.

Second turn

First turn

❹ Twist the top of the hand toward the body. Pick up the second turn lying over the back of the hand.

First turn

Second turn

Thumb holds rope

Turk's Head: side view

❺ **Cross** the second turn over the first at the back of the hand. Hold your thumb over the crossed strands in the palm of the hand to keep them in place.

First turn

Working end

Second turn

Turk's Head: overview

❻ **Twist** the back of the hand toward the body. Tuck the working end over the second turn, then under the first turn, and pull through. The formation of the three-strand braid is now visible.

Working end

Outer right strand

Standing part

❼ **Turn** the palm of the hand towards the body. Pick up the working end, take it behind the standing part, then tuck it up through the outer right strand below the crossed rope of the first turn.

❽ **Double** (p. 25) the Turk's Head, following the first cycle of tucks with the working end, and ensuring that the strands do not cross. If the finished knot is to be free-standing, *seize* (p. 25) the ends of the rope inside the knot.

TURK'S HEAD – FOUR-LEAD FIVE-BIGHT

This Turk's Head is based on a continuous four-strand *braid*. Estimate (p. 22) the length of rope needed for this knot before starting, and continually adjust the *eyes* between the strands so that they are even.

Working end

❶ Pass the *working end* over the palm and around one hand. Take it across the *standing part*, then pass it back under the standing part, leaving a diamond-shaped eye in the center of the palm.

Eye

Palm faces body

Standing part

Working end

❷ Take the working end around the back of the hand, and bring it up at the front to the left of the standing part.

Standing part

Working end

❸ Tuck the working end up through the diamond-shaped eye from back to front.

Eye

❹ Twist the top of the hand toward the body. Continue to weave a braid by tucking the working end over and under the two strands lying on the back of the hand. Leave a gap with two eyes between the working end and the left strand.

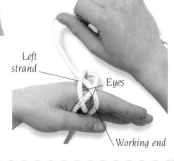

Left strand

Eyes

Working end

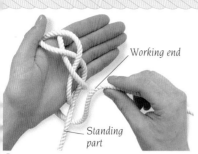

❺ Twist the palm of the hand back toward the body. Bring the working end underneath the hand and over the standing part from right to left.

Working end

Standing part

Turk's Head: side view

Working end

strands of ?ected eye

❻ Weave the working end diagonally from left to right under, over, then under the three strands of the bisected diamond-shaped eye.

Turk's Head: overview

Outer left strand

Working end

Eyes

❼ Working from right to left, weave the working end diagonally over and under the next two strands at the top of the hand. Adjust the crossed strands so that the eyes between them are of equal size.

Working end

Fourth strand of plait

Standing part

❽ Take the working end over the outer left strand to form a final eye. Turn the back of the hand toward the body, and start to double (p. 25) the knot. Trim and *seize* (p. 25) the ends of the rope.

Outer left strand

Eye

63

TURK'S HEAD –
FIVE-LEAD FOUR-BIGHT

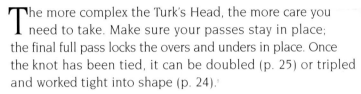

The more complex the Turk's Head, the more care you need to take. Make sure your passes stay in place; the final full pass locks the overs and unders in place. Once the knot has been tied, it can be doubled (p. 25) or tripled and worked tight into shape (p. 24).

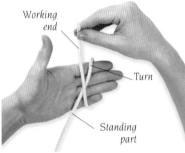

❶ Estimate (p. 22) the amount of the rope needed for the knot. Pass the *working end* over the top of the hand to make a *turn*. Then cross it over the *standing part* from right to left.

❷ Make a second turn around the hand to the right of the first turn. Cross the working end over the first turn from left to right.

❸ Tuck the working end through the first turn at the top of the hand.

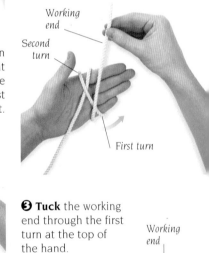

❹ Make a third turn around the hand between the first and second turns, and tuck the working end parallel to the standing part, passing under and over the strands from left to right.

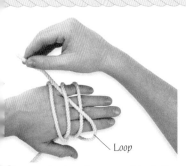

Turk's Head: side view

5 Turn the hand over and tuck the working end over, under, and over the three strands from right to left. Do not lose the loop that has formed around your index finger.

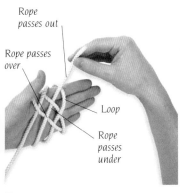

Rope passes out

Rope passes over

Loop

Rope passes under

Turk's Head: overview

6 Turn the palm of the hand toward the body. Bring the working end up to the right of the standing part, and tuck it from left to right, passing over, under, and out through the loop you had saved.

Rope passes over

Rope passes under

Rope passes under

7 Turn the hand over, and tuck the working end of the rope from right to left, passing under, over, and under the strands.

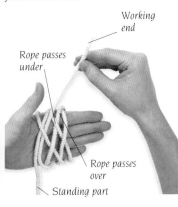

Working end

Rope passes under

Rope passes over

Standing part

8 Turn the hand back again. Tuck the working end parallel to the standing part, going under and over the strands. Double the knot (p. 25), and *seize* the ends of the rope (p. 25).

Hunter's Bend, p. 72

Tucked Sheet Bend, p. 69

Double Sheet Bend, p. 68

Fisherman's Knot, p. 74

Double Fisherman's Knot, p. 75

Water Knot, p. 77

Sheet
Bend,
p. 68

Rope Yarn
Knot, p. 70

Ashley's Bend, p. 73

BENDS

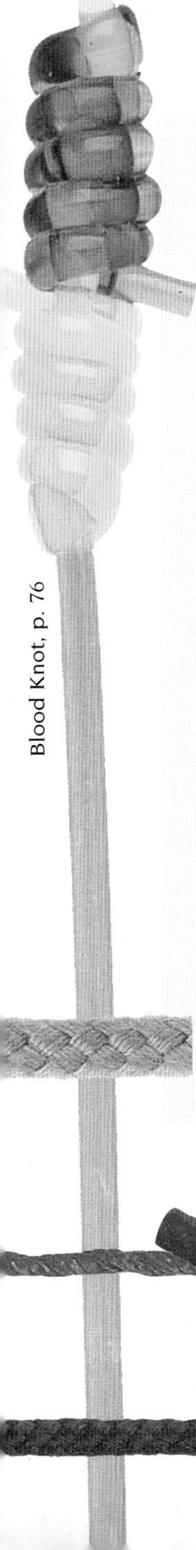

Blood Knot, p. 76

Lanyard Knot, p. 71

A bend is used to join two lengths of rope together temporarily. For most bends, the ropes need to be of equal size in order to tie a secure knot. A few bends are suitable for joining ropes of different sizes. As with all knots subject to strain, leave the ends of a bend long enough so that they do not work loose when the knot is tightened under load. A good bend can be easily untied, even after being put under considerable strain, except when it has been tied in fine line.

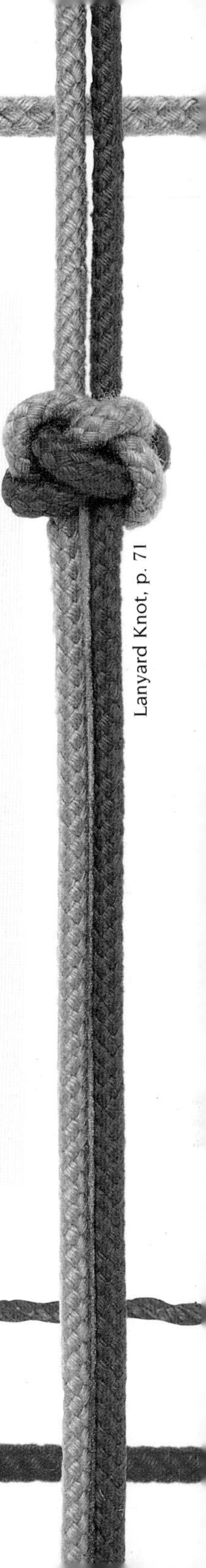

Carrick Bend, p. 71

SHEET BEND

Quick and easy to tie, the Sheet Bend is one of the most commonly used knots for joining two ropes. If the ropes are of unequal diameter, it is preferable to tie a Double Sheet Bend (below).

Working end
Loop

❶ **Fold** the end of a length of rope back on itself to form a *loop*. Pass the *working end* of a second rope up through the loop.

Workin end

First rope

❷ **Pass** the working end of the second rope around the short end of the loop, then behind the first rope.

Short end of loop

Long end of loop

Rope ends lie on same side of knot

❸ **Bring** the working end to the front of the knot, passing it over the long end of the loop, then take it under itself.

DOUBLE SHEET BEND

Complete Steps 1–3 of the Sheet Bend (above), using a thin rope as the *working end*. Pass the working end around the *loop* and under itself a second time. Pull tight to secure the knot.

Standing part

Loop

❹ **To** finish, pull on the loop and on the *standing part* of the second length of rope, locking the knot in place. Trim (p. 25) the working end if required, and *seize* (p. 25) the two ends together.

TUCKED SHEET BEND

This variation of the Sheet Bend is useful because the ends are tucked against the rope. This ensures that they do not snag if pulled along.

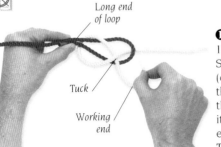

Long end of loop

Tuck

Working end

❶ Follow Steps 1 and 2 from the Sheet Bend (opposite). Bring the *working end* to the front, passing it over the long end of the *loop*. Tuck it under itself.

Working end

Bight

Standing part

❷ Fold the working end back on itself, passing it over the standing part. Tuck it under the *bight* formed by the *tuck* made in Step 1, creating a figure eight.

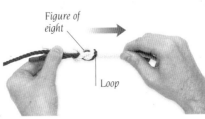

Figure of eight

Loop

❸ Hold the ends, and pull the standing part so that the figure eight sits neatly on top of the loop.

SLIPPED SHEET BEND

Complete Step 1 of the Tucked Sheet Bend (above). Rather than tucking the *working end* in Step 2, tuck a generous-sized *bight* of the rope under the bight formed by the *tuck* in Step 1 while creating a figure eight. Pull tight to make sure the bight is securely trapped.

ROPE YARN KNOT

In the past, sailors would take the best *yarns* from old rope and remake them into twice-laid *cordage* by using this knot. It can also be used for joining knitting yarn and other materials used in textile projects, and is similar to the Reef Knot (p. 48). The instructions below are for *Z-laid* yarn (p. 10). For *S-laid* yarn (p. 10), the knot should be tied in a mirror version.

Right yarn

Left yarn

❶ Divide the fibers that make up each of the yarns into two halves. Interlink the lower half of the right yarn behind the lower half of the left yarn, and the upper half of the right yarn over the upper half of the left yarn.

❷ Push the interlinked ends close together, but keep the lower halves of the yarns distinct. These are the left and right *working ends* that will form the knot. Leave the other half-yarns static and parallel to the rope yarn.

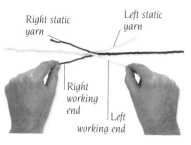

Right static yarn

Left static yarn

Right working end

Left working end

Left working end

Right working end

❸ Bring the left working end up behind the right yarn and the left static, and the right working end up over the left yarn and the right static. Now cross the right working end over the left working end.

❹ Tuck the right working end behind and up through the loop formed by the left working end. Pull both the ends to secure the knot.

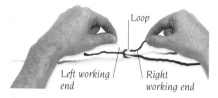

Loop

Left working end

Right working end

CARRICK BEND

This is the knot to use when joining heavy *cable*. It also works well for rope and *line*, and can be allowed to tighten and collapse on itself when strain is taken on the *standing parts*.

❶ Make a *crossing turn* with a rope. Pass the *working end* of a second rope under the *standing part* and over the working end of the first rope.

Working end of second rope

Crossing turn

Working end of first rope lies over standing part

Standing part

Turn

❷ Bring the working end of the second rope up through the turn and over itself. Tuck it down through the turn, and pull on all four ends to tighten the knot.

Working end

LANYARD KNOT

Tucking the *working ends* through the middle of the Carrick Bend (above) produces a knot that can be used as a key fob, zipper pull, or whistle strap.

❶ Complete Steps 1–2 of the Carrick Bend. Turn the knot over. Take the *working end* of the first rope over the *standing part* of the second rope, and tuck it through the *eye* at the center of the knot.

First standing part

Eye

First working end

Second standing part

❷ In the same way, take the working end of the second rope over the standing part of the first, then tuck it up through the center of the knot.

Second working end

Working ends

❸ To tighten the knot, pull on the standing parts against the working ends. Work the knot into shape (p. 24) with the fingers or a *marlingspike*.

HUNTER'S BEND

The Hunter's Bend can be used instead of the Sheet Bend (p. 68) to join lengths of slippery synthetic rope. Previously known as the Rigger's Knot, it acquired its new name when it appeared on the front page of *The London Times* in 1978, credited to Dr. Edward Hunter. This publicity for a knot also led to the foundation of the International Guild of Knot Tyers (p. 176).

Upper working end

❶ **Overlap** the *working ends* of two ropes, and lay them side by side.

Lower working end

❷ **Form** a *crossing turn* with the doubled working ends, twisting the strands held in the right hand behind the strands held in the left hand.

Upper working end

Crossing turn

Upper working end

Lower working end

❸ **Tuck** the upper working end now held in the left hand through the crossing turn from back to front. Tuck the lower working end held in the right hand through the crossing turn from front to back.

❹ **Making** sure that the working ends remain tucked through the turn, pull on the *standing parts* to tighten the knot.

Standing part

Standing part

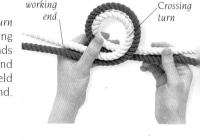

ASHLEY'S BEND

Ashley's Bend is easily untied, yet it is also one of the most secure bends, even when subjected to a lot of movement. It is particularly useful for tying a bend in *thin line*.

❶ **Make** a *crossing turn*, bringing the *working end* of a rope behind the *standing part*.

Working end

Crossing turn

Standing part

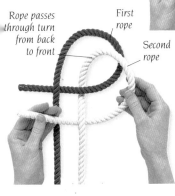

Rope passes through turn from back to front

First rope

Second rope

❷ **Make** a crossing turn with the second rope in the same way, first passing the working end through the first crossing turn. Lay the working end of the second rope over the standing part of the first.

Working ends

❸ **Hold** the two crossing turns together, then pass the working ends up through both turns from front to back.

Working ends

❹ **Start** to tighten the knot by pulling on the working ends and on the standing parts.

Standing parts

❺ **Finish** tightening the knot by separating the standing parts, then pulling on each one.

Standing parts are separated

FISHERMAN'S KNOT

The Fisherman's Knot, made up of two Overhand Knots (p. 28), is a simple yet effective knot for tying together two ropes or *lines* of small and equal diameter. It is a favorite with anglers and climbers, who sometimes tape down the ends (below) to prevent them from working loose. The short ends of the finished knot must be at least five times the diameter of the rope.

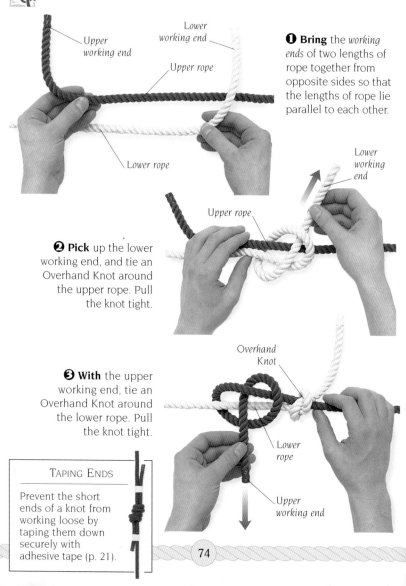

Upper working end

Lower working end

Upper rope

Lower rope

❶ Bring the *working ends* of two lengths of rope together from opposite sides so that the lengths of rope lie parallel to each other.

Lower working end

Upper rope

❷ Pick up the lower working end, and tie an Overhand Knot around the upper rope. Pull the knot tight.

Overhand Knot

❸ With the upper working end, tie an Overhand Knot around the lower rope. Pull the knot tight.

Lower rope

Upper working end

TAPING ENDS

Prevent the short ends of a knot from working loose by taping them down securely with adhesive tape (p. 21).

Knots slide together

❹ Pull on each length of rope so that the two Overhand Knots slide together and lie snugly against each other. The finished knot may be secured by taping down the working ends (opposite).

DOUBLE FISHERMAN'S KNOT

When using rope or *line* that is particularly slippery, tie a Double Fisherman's Knot to make sure that the knot does not come undone when it is put under strain.

❶ Follow Step 1 of the Fisherman's Knot (opposite). With the lower *working end*, make two *turns* around the upper rope. Pass the lower working end through the turns. Pull the knot tight.

Lower working end

Turns

Upper rope

Turns

Lower rope

Upper working end

❷ Tie another knot by taking the upper working end and tucking it through two turns made around the lower rope. Pull the knot tight. Finish tying the knot as for Step 4 of the Fisherman's Knot.

BLOOD KNOT

Also known as the Barrel Knot, the Blood Knot is most effective when used to join *thin lines* of equal diameter. It is favored by anglers for joining nylon line, which can be moistened with saliva to help draw the knot tight. The Blood Knot can withstand a large amount of strain, but will subsequently be almost impossible to untie.

❶ **Overlap** the ends of two lengths of line. Pass the *working end* of the upper line around the lower line to form a *turn*.

Upper working en

Lower line *Upper line*

Turn

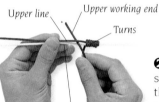

Upper line *Upper working end*

Turns

Lower line

❷ **Make** approximately five turns side by side around the upper and the lower lines to bind them together. Pass the upper working end up between the two lengths of line.

❸ **With** the lower working end, make a turn around the upper line about 2½ in (8 cm) away from the previous set of turns.

Lower working end *Turns*

Upper line

Turns *Lower working end*

❹ **Make** the same number of turns around the upper and lower lines with the lower working end. Then pass it down between the two lengths of line.

Short working ends can be trimmed (p. 25)

❺ **To** tighten the knot, pull on both lines so that the two sets of round turns lie neatly together.

WATER KNOT

Also known as the Double Overhand Bend or Tape Knot, the Water Knot is strong and reliable. It is the recommended knot for joining flat *tape*, such as that used by climbers. Make sure that the second strand of tape or rope always remains on the same side of the first strand as the knot is doubled (p. 25).

❶ Tie a loose Overhand Knot (p. 28) at the end of a first length of rope, taking the *working end* over the *standing part*.

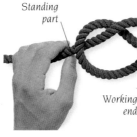

Standing part

Overhand Knot

Working end

Second working end

Overhand Knot

First rope

❷ With the working end of a second rope, follow the end of the first rope into the Overhand Knot, and start to double the knot.

❸ Continue to follow the path of the Overhand Knot with the second working end. Make sure that the second rope does not cross over the first.

Second working end

Ropes do not cross

❹ To tighten the Water Knot, pull on the ropes on either side of the knot. Work the knot into shape (p. 24).

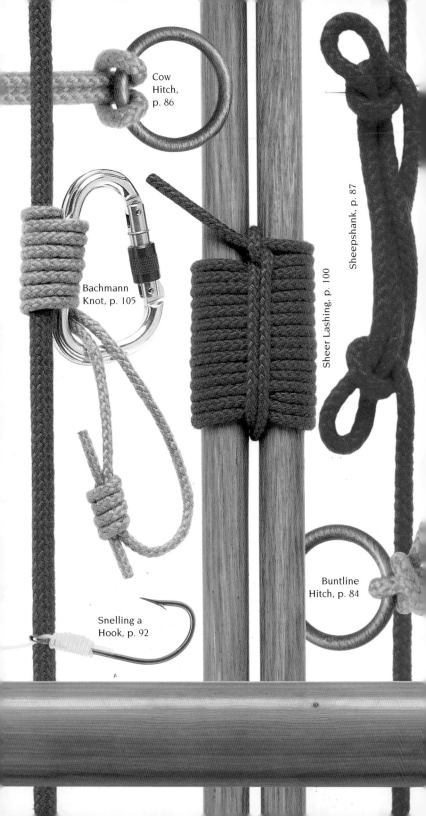

Cow
Hitch,
p. 86

Sheepshank, p. 87

Bachmann
Knot, p. 105

Sheer Lashing, p. 100

Snelling a
Hook, p. 92

Buntline
Hitch, p. 84

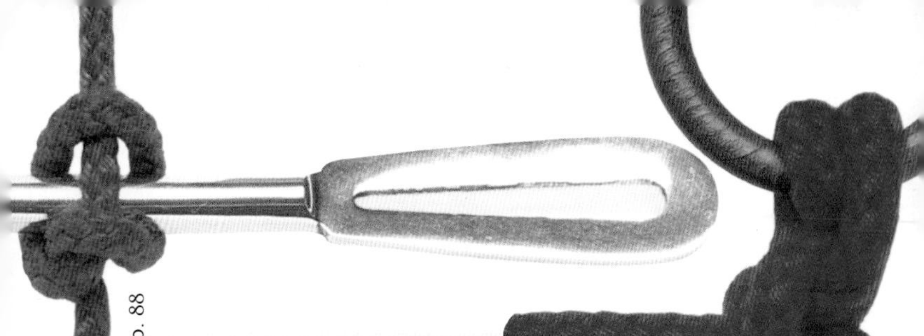

Marlingspike Hitch, p. 88

Palomar Knot, p. 95

Round Turn & Two Half-Hitches, p. 83

HITCHES

A hitch is used to tie a rope to or around an object, often a pole, a ring, or another rope. Some hitches are designed to be tied quickly, particularly those used by sailors, while others can be untied with a brief tug on one end. When choosing a hitch for a particular task, check that it is suitable for taking strain in the direction required, and make sure that tension is applied to the correct end of the rope once the knot is tied.

Highwayman's
Hitch, p. 89

Italian
Hitch,
p. 107

Fisherman's Bend, p. 85

Sheepshank Man o' War, p. 87

Improved Clinch Knot, p. 94

Prusik Knot, p. 104

Square Lashing, p. 96

Pedigree Cow Hitch, p. 86

Rolling Hitch,
p. 82

Cow Hitch
with Toggle,
p. 86

Clinch Knot, p. 94

Icicle Hitch, p. 102

Diagonal
Lashing,
p. 98

Klemheist
Knot, p. 106

ROLLING HITCH

This knot is used to tie a rope to a pole, or to take strain off another rope. Strain can be applied sideways to this knot in one direction. To apply strain in the opposite direction, tie a mirror version of the knot (below).

❶ Make a *turn* around a pole, bringing the *working end* up on the right side of the *standing part*. Take the working end across the standing part.

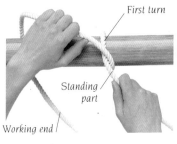

First turn

Standing part

Working end

❷ Make a second turn around the pole, bringing the working end up between the second turn and the standing part.

Second turn locks first turn in place

Working end

Standing part

Working end   Third turn

Standing part

❸ Make a third turn beside the second and across the first. Bring the working end up on the left side of the standing part. Tuck the working end under the third turn.

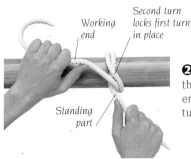

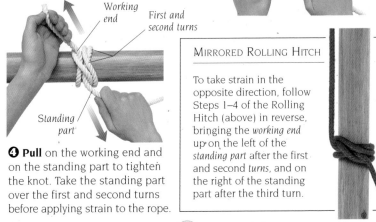

Working end

First and second turns

Standing part

❹ Pull on the working end and on the standing part to tighten the knot. Take the standing part over the first and second turns before applying strain to the rope.

MIRRORED ROLLING HITCH

To take strain in the opposite direction, follow Steps 1–4 of the Rolling Hitch (above) in reverse, bringing the *working end* up on the left of the *standing part* after the first and second *turns*, and on the right of the standing part after the third turn.

ROUND TURN & TWO HALF-HITCHES

This knot can be used to secure a rope to a pole or ring in a variety of situations, from mooring a boat to tying a clothesline. Even if placed under a great deal of strain, it can still be untied fairly easily. The initial *round turn* takes any strain that is applied to the knot, and the two *half-hitches* keep the knot in place.

❶ **Bring** the *working end* up through a ring from back to front. Pass the working end through the ring a second time to form a *round turn*.

Round turn

Working end

First half-hitch

Working end

❷ **Take** the working end across then behind the *standing part*. Bring it to the front of the knot again, and tuck it behind itself to form a half-hitch.

Second half hitch

Working end

Standing part

Standing part

❸ **Make** a second half-hitch, taking the working end under the standing part, around to the front, and tucking it behind itself. Pull on the working end and on the standing part to tighten the knot.

BUNTLINE HITCH

The Buntline Hitch will not come undone, even when subjected to a lot of movement. On square-sailed ships, it was used to secure a line to the Bunt (the middle part of a sail). It can also be used without a ring as a simple knot for a necktie.

❶ Pass a *working end* of a rope through a ring from back to front. Take the working end behind the *standing part* to form a half-hitch. Bring the working end across the front of the half-hitch.

Working end

Half hitch

Standing part

Half hitch

Working end

❷ Take the working end to the back of the knot and behind the half-hitch.

Half hitch

Working end

Standing part

Working end

❸ Bring the working end to the front of the knot, then pass it down through the half-hitch.

❹ Pull on the standing part and working end to tighten the Buntline Hitch.

FISHERMAN'S BEND

This hitch, also called the Anchor Bend, is ideal for securing a rope to an anchor or a buoy. It is similar to the Round Turn and Two Half-hitches (p. 83), with the first *half-hitch* locked in place by the *round turn*. For additional security, *seize* (p. 168) the short *working end* to the *standing part*.

❶ Pass the *working end* of a rope twice through a ring from back to front to form a *round turn*.

Round turn

Working end

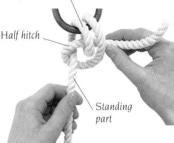

Round turn

Half hitch

Standing part

❷ Bring the working end down and behind the *standing part*. Tuck it through the round turn to form a locking half-hitch around the standing part.

Half hitch

❸ Make a second half-hitch, taking the working end behind then in front of the standing part, and tucking it under itself. Tighten the knot by pulling on the standing part and on the working end.

Standing part

85

COW HITCH

A lso called the Lark's Head, the Cow Hitch can be made through a ring or around a pole. Essentially composed of two *half-hitches* tied in opposite directions, this is the least secure of all hitches. Equal strain needs to be applied to both *standing parts* to make sure that the knot is secure.

❶ **Double** a length of rope to form a *bight*. Pass the bight up through a ring from back to front. Widen the bight to extend either side of the *standing parts*.

Bight

❷ **Pull** the standing parts forward through the bight. Pull tight.

Standing parts

PEDIGREE COW HITCH

I f only one *standing part* of a Cow Hitch (above) is taking strain, tie a Pedigree Cow Hitch, tucking the second standing part between the *bight* and the ring to secure the knot.

COW HITCH WITH TOGGLE

T his variation of the Cow Hitch (above) is used when the two ends of the rope are fixed, and only the *bight* can be passed through the ring. Complete Step 1 as for the Cow Hitch. Insert the toggle over the first strand of the bight, under the two *standing parts*, and over the second strand of the bight. Pull on the standing parts to secure the toggle in the knot. The toggle may have a tail of rope so that it can be pulled out to undo the knot.

SHEEPSHANK

The Sheepshank is designed to shorten a rope before use. It can also be used to relieve strain on a worn part of a rope by positioning the damaged strands in the center of the knot (p. 17).

❶ Make three *crossing turns* all in the same direction.

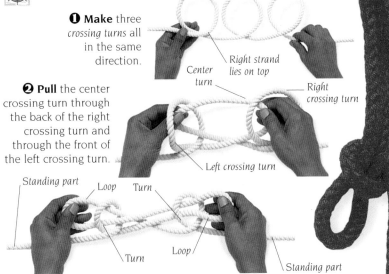

Center turn

Right strand lies on top

Right crossing turn

❷ Pull the center crossing turn through the back of the right crossing turn and through the front of the left crossing turn.

Left crossing turn

Standing part   Loop   Turn

Turn

Loop

Turn

Standing part

❸ Pull on the newly formed *loops*, then on the *standing parts* so that the outer crossing turns tighten around the loops. The knot will hold only if strain is applied to the standing parts.

SHEEPSHANK MAN O' WAR

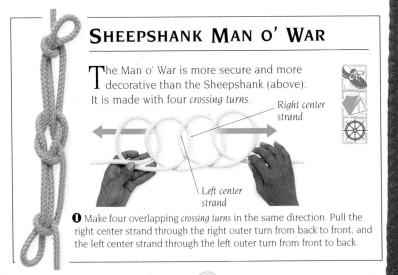

The Man o' War is more secure and more decorative than the Sheepshank (above). It is made with four *crossing turns*.

Right center strand

Left center strand

❶ Make four overlapping *crossing turns* in the same direction. Pull the right center strand through the right outer turn from back to front, and the left center strand through the left outer turn from front to back.

MARLINGSPIKE HITCH

Originally used by sailors, the Marlingspike Hitch allows *thin line* or rope to be pulled without it biting into the hand. Instead of a *marlingspike*, any long tool, such as a screwdriver or a spanner, can be used. Once the knot is no longer needed, remove the tool and the hitch will disappear.

Fixed end of rope

❶ Lay a marlingspike on top of a length of rope fixed at one end. Lift the rope upward over the marlingspike, then twist the marlingspike upward in a clockwise direction.

Marlingspike

Standing part

Hold strands at crossing point

Crossing turn

❷ Lift the *crossing turn* that has formed around the marlingspike up toward the *standing part*. Insert the tip of the marlingspike behind the standing part.

Crossing turn

Standing part

❸ Spread the turn to cover both sides of the standing part.

Standing part

Marlingspike provides handhold

❹ Pull the standing part through the crossing turn with the point of the marlingspike. Push the marlingspike farther into the knot.

❺ To put strain on the rope, pull downward on either side of the marlingspike with one or both hands.

HIGHWAYMAN'S HITCH

As the name suggests, this knot is often used to tether horses and release them quickly. Ensure that strain is applied to the standing part – strain, or a quick pull, on the other end will untie the knot. Use this hitch to release a dinghy from a high mooring ring.

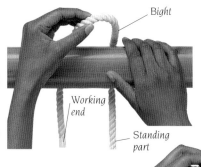

Bight

Working end

Standing part

❶ **Double** the end of a length of rope to form a *bight*, then pass the rope behind a pole.

Second bight

First bight

❷ **Form** a second bight with the *standing part*, then insert it through the first bight from front to back.

Working end

Second bight

❸ **Pull** tight on the *working end* to lock the second bight in place. Double the working end to form a third bight.

Standing part

Third bight

Working end can be pulled to release knot

Standing part

❹ **Insert** the third bight through the second from front to back, then pull hard on the standing part to lock the knot in place. Strain can now be taken on the standing part.

WAGGONER'S HITCH

The Waggoner's Hitch acts as a lever, allowing strain to be put on a length of rope so that loads can be lashed down very tightly. The hitch comes undone as soon as the strain is released, so the knot needs to be properly formed and locked in place. Employed for centuries to secure loads onto wagons, it is still used by truck drivers. The Waggoner's Hitch can cause severe *chafe* on a rope if the knot is used repeatedly in the same place on the rope.

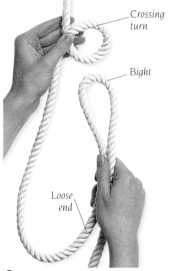

Crossing turn

Bight

Loose end

❶ Ensure that the rope is fixed in position at one end. Make a *crossing turn* in the middle of the rope, with the upper strand of the crossing turn lying on top. Form a *bight* with the loose end, leaving a long length of rope between the crossing turn and the bight.

❷ Insert the bight up through the crossing turn from back to front. Pull on the *loop* that has now formed between the crossing turn and the bight to tighten the turn around the bight.

Hold bight in place

Crossing turn

Bight

Loop

Loop

Twists

❸ Make two twists in the loop toward the bight and the crossing turn. Make sure that the bight and the turn remain locked in place.

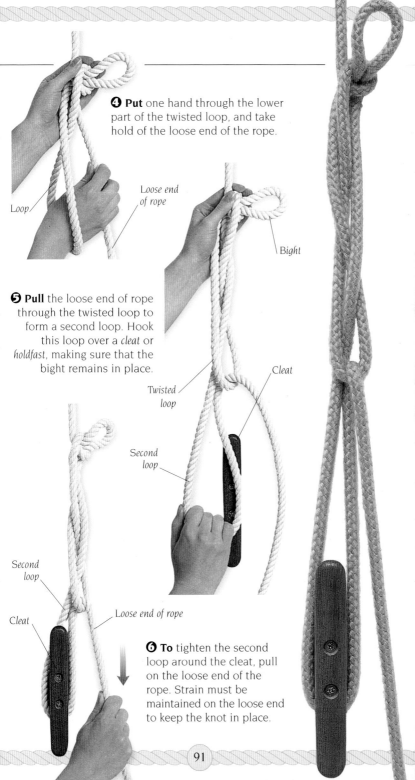

❹ **Put** one hand through the lower part of the twisted loop, and take hold of the loose end of the rope.

Loose end of rope

Loop

Bight

❺ **Pull** the loose end of rope through the twisted loop to form a second loop. Hook this loop over a *cleat* or *holdfast*, making sure that the bight remains in place.

Twisted loop

Cleat

Second loop

Second loop

Cleat

Loose end of rope

❻ **To** tighten the second loop around the cleat, pull on the loose end of the rope. Strain must be maintained on the loose end to keep the knot in place.

SNELLING A HOOK

This knot binds a *line* to a hook with many *turns*. When tying the knot with monofilament nylon fishing line (p. 13), moisten the line before pulling the knot tight to help the turns slide snugly on top of one another. This method can also be used to tie a line to a hook with a *spade end*.

❶ With the point of a hook uppermost, pass the end of a line up through the *eye* of the hook. Pull the line through. Form a large *crossing turn*, taking the line over itself just above the eye. This is the crossing point. Leave a short tail of line below the crossing point. Hold the lower part of the crossing turn parallel to the shank of the hook.

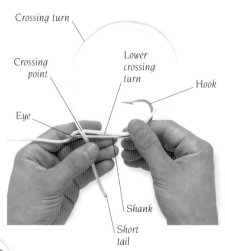

Crossing turn

Crossing point

Eye

Lower crossing turn

Hook

Shank

Short tail

Upper crossing turn

Crossing point

Short tail

❷ Hold the short tail parallel to the shank of the hook, keeping the lower part of the crossing turn parallel to the shank at the same time. Take hold of the upper part of the crossing turn above the crossing point.

Short tail

Lower crossing turn

Upper crossing turn

❸ Keeping the two parts of the line parallel to the shank of the hook, start to wrap the upper part of the crossing turn behind the shank. Bring it to the front of the hook, keeping the crossing turn open so that it can pass over the point of the hook.

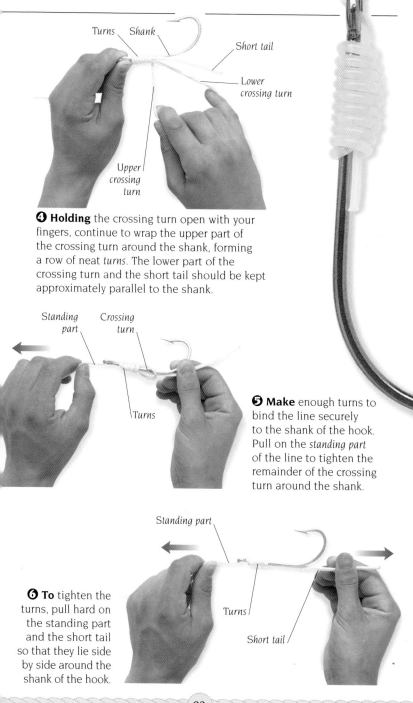

4 Holding the crossing turn open with your fingers, continue to wrap the upper part of the crossing turn around the shank, forming a row of neat *turns*. The lower part of the crossing turn and the short tail should be kept approximately parallel to the shank.

5 Make enough turns to bind the line securely to the shank of the hook. Pull on the *standing part* of the line to tighten the remainder of the crossing turn around the shank.

6 To tighten the turns, pull hard on the standing part and the short tail so that they lie side by side around the shank of the hook.

CLINCH KNOT

The Clinch Knot can be tied quickly and is one of the easiest knots to use for attaching monofilament nylon fishing *line* (p. 13) to the *eye* of a hook. To help the *turns* tighten snugly on top of each other, moisten the monofilament nylon line before working the knot into shape (p. 24).

❶ Pass the end of a line twice through the eye of a hook to make a loose *round turn*, leaving a long *working end*.

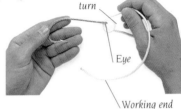

Round turn

Eye

Working end

Turns   Standing part

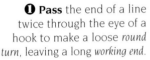

Working end

❷ Wrap the working end around the *standing part* to make five or six *turns*.

Working end

❸ Pass the working end through the round turn.

Short end

Turns

Standing part

Round turn

Eye

❹ Pull on the hook and on the standing part, tightening the turns so that they lie snugly against the eye of the hook. Work the knot into shape, and trim (p. 25) the short end if required.

IMPROVED CLINCH KNOT

If a monofilament fishing *line* is particularly fine or slippery, make an extra *tuck* to tie an Improved Clinch Knot, which will prevent the knot from working loose.

Eye   Working end

❶ Complete Steps 1–3 of the Clinch Knot (above), tucking the working end through the eye that has formed between the working end and the turns. Pull tight, and trim (p. 25) as in Step 4.

PALOMAR KNOT

Use the Palomar Knot to tie a fishing *line* to a hook when the line is likely to take a great deal of strain. It is suitable for all types of fishing line. Moisten the line for a neater finish to the knot.

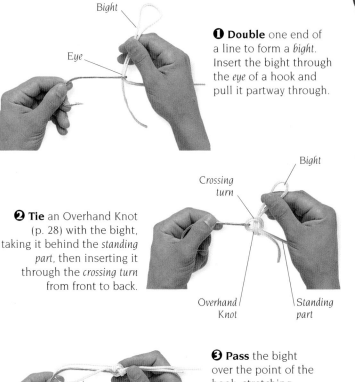

Bight

Eye

❶ Double one end of a line to form a *bight*. Insert the bight through the *eye* of a hook and pull it partway through.

Bight

Crossing turn

❷ Tie an Overhand Knot (p. 28) with the bight, taking it behind the *standing part*, then inserting it through the *crossing turn* from front to back.

Overhand Knot

Standing part

❸ Pass the bight over the point of the hook, stretching the line if necessary.

Bight

Point

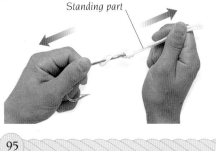

Standing part

❹ Pull on the hook and on the standing part to tighten the knot, moistening the line with saliva to help it slide into place. Work the knot into shape (p. 24).

SQUARE LASHING

A *lashing* is used to bind two poles together with rope. The Square Lashing is used to hold two poles at a 90-degree angle to one another. To make this lashing as secure as possible, it is important to tighten each *turn* as it is made. *Frapping turns* stabilize the lashing and tighten it further.

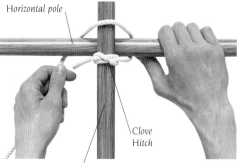

Horizontal pole

Clove Hitch

Vertical pole

❶ Tie a Clove Hitch (p. 56) to the lower part of a vertical pole laid in front of a horizontal pole. Wind the rope alternately behind then in front of the next two sections of pole.

❷ Pull on the rope to tighten it around the poles. The Clove Hitch will slip to one side of the vertical pole.

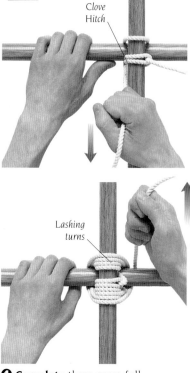

Clove Hitch

Lashing turns

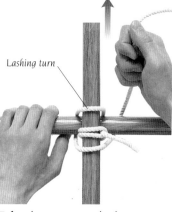

Lashing turn

❸ Take the rope over the lower part of the vertical pole then under the next section of the horizontal pole to complete the first *lashing turn*. Pull the rope tight.

❹ Complete three more full lashing turns around the poles. Pull each one tight as it is made.

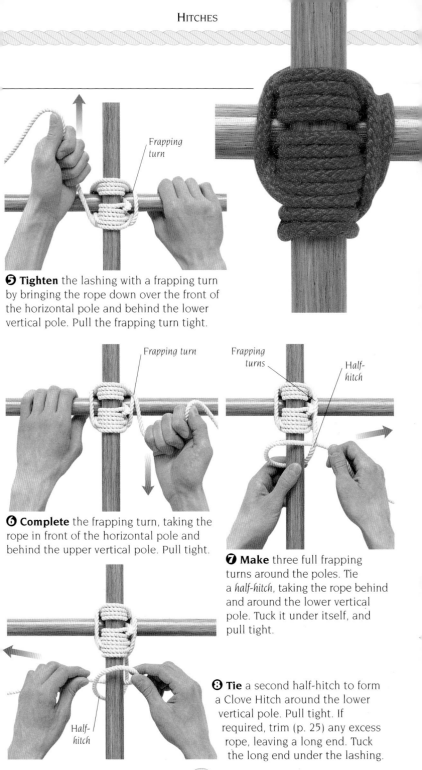

❺ Tighten the lashing with a frapping turn by bringing the rope down over the front of the horizontal pole and behind the lower vertical pole. Pull the frapping turn tight.

Frapping turn

❻ Complete the frapping turn, taking the rope in front of the horizontal pole and behind the upper vertical pole. Pull tight.

Frapping turn

Frapping turns

Half-hitch

❼ Make three full frapping turns around the poles. Tie a *half-hitch*, taking the rope behind and around the lower vertical pole. Tuck it under itself, and pull tight.

Half-hitch

❽ Tie a second half-hitch to form a Clove Hitch around the lower vertical pole. Pull tight. If required, trim (p. 25) any excess rope, leaving a long end. Tuck the long end under the lashing.

DIAGONAL LASHING

This is the ideal *lashing* for securing diagonal *braces* used to hold a structure rigid. When wooden poles are used for scaffolding, a combination of Diagonal and Square Lashings (p. 96) is used to hold them together. Make sure that you have enough rope (p. 22) to complete the lashing.

Working end

Timber Hitch

Turns lock Timber Hitch in place

❶ Tie a Timber Hitch (p. 58) horizontally around two poles crossed diagonally. Pull tight. Take the *working end* around to the back of the poles in preparation for the first *turn*.

❷ Make three full horizontal turns around both poles and over the Timber Hitch. Pull each turn tight as it is made.

❸ Change the direction of the turns by taking the rope behind the poles at the bottom of the lashing, then to the front of the poles at the top.

Third turn is pulled tight

Third turn is completed before direction is changed

❹ Make three vertical turns around the crossed poles, tightening each turn before making the next one.

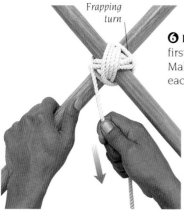

Frapping turn

❺ Tighten the lashing with a *frapping turn* by threading the rope alternately behind then in front of each pole. This will help to secure the lashing.

Frapping turn

❻ Pull the rope tight to complete the first frapping turn around the lashing. Make two more frapping turns, pulling each one tight as it is completed.

❼ Tie a *half-hitch* around one of the lower poles. Slide the half-hitch up the pole against the lashing, then pull it tight from below.

Half-hitch

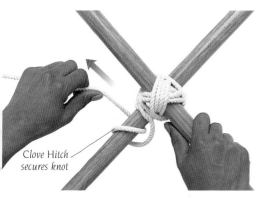

❽ To form a finishing Clove Hitch (p. 56), tie a second half-hitch and pull it tight against the lashing. Trim the rope (p. 25), leaving a short end to prevent the knot from working loose.

Clove Hitch secures knot

SHEER LASHING

This *lashing* is often used to bind adjacent poles together. It is also an effective way of adding reinforcing timber to the side of a weak or broken pole. The *frapping turns*, used to tighten the lashing, may be left out and replaced with wedges inserted between the poles. A loose Sheer Lashing made around the ends of two poles will allow the poles to be opened out and used as an A-frame (below right).

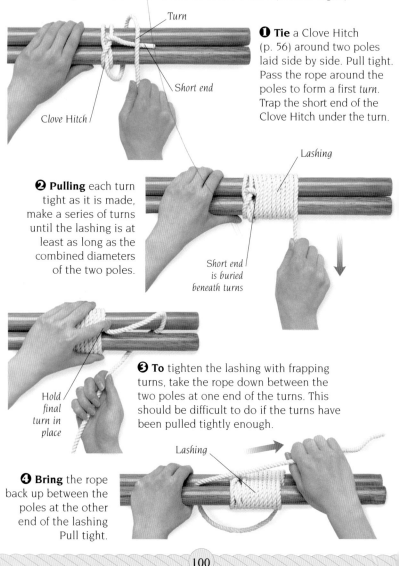

Turn

Short end

Clove Hitch

❶ **Tie** a Clove Hitch (p. 56) around two poles laid side by side. Pull tight. Pass the rope around the poles to form a first *turn*. Trap the short end of the Clove Hitch under the turn.

Lashing

❷ **Pulling** each turn tight as it is made, make a series of turns until the lashing is at least as long as the combined diameters of the two poles.

Short end is buried beneath turns

Hold final turn in place

❸ **To** tighten the lashing with frapping turns, take the rope down between the two poles at one end of the turns. This should be difficult to do if the turns have been pulled tightly enough.

Lashing

❹ **Bring** the rope back up between the poles at the other end of the lashing Pull tight.

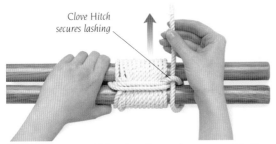

Frapping turn

Half-hitch

❺ **Take** the rope twice across each side of the lashing to complete two full frapping turns. Pass the rope once more between the poles, then around one pole. Tuck it under itself to form a *half-hitch*.

Clove Hitch secures lashing

❻ **Pull** the first half-hitch tight. Make a second half-hitch, forming a finishing Clove Hitch, by taking the rope around the same pole, and tucking it under itself. Pull tight, and trim (p. 25) the end of the rope.

TYING AN A-FRAME LASHING

Also known as "Sheer Legs," an A-Frame Lashing is made in the same way as a Sheer Lashing (opposite), with the *lashing* and *frapping turns* made slightly loose so that the poles can be opened out. It is often used to raise a boat mast or to form the legs of a rope bridge, although care must be taken that the feet of the frame do not slip.

ICICLE HITCH

W hen properly adjusted, this special hitch has strong holding power and a much better grip than the Rolling Hitch (p. 82). For very smooth surfaces, make more *turns*, and hold the knot in place with your hand as strain is applied until the hitch has held.

❶ Make a *turn* around a rod, taking the *working end* to the left of the *standing part*. Cross it over the standing part.

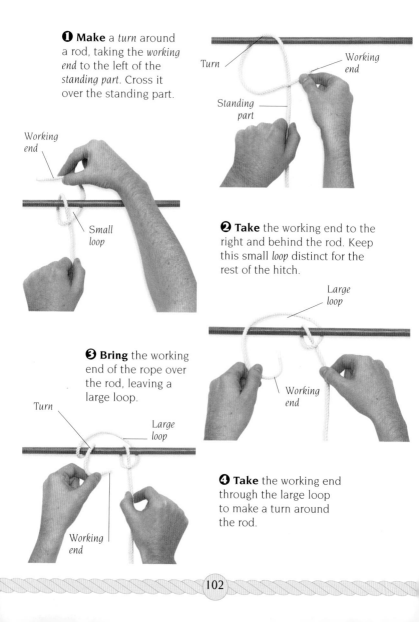

Turn

Working end

Standing part

Working end

Small loop

❷ Take the working end to the right and behind the rod. Keep this small *loop* distinct for the rest of the hitch.

Large loop

❸ Bring the working end of the rope over the rod, leaving a large loop.

Turn

Large loop

Working end

Working end

❹ Take the working end through the large loop to make a turn around the rod.

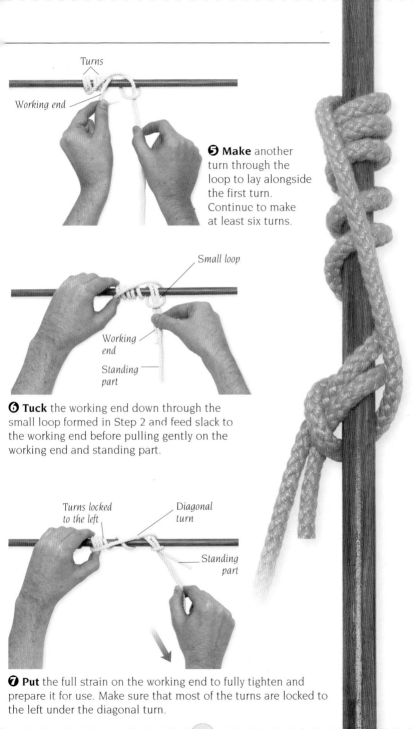

Turns

Working end

❺ Make another turn through the loop to lay alongside the first turn. Continue to make at least six turns.

Small loop

Working end

Standing part

❻ Tuck the working end down through the small loop formed in Step 2 and feed slack to the working end before pulling gently on the working end and standing part.

Turns locked to the left

Diagonal turn

Standing part

❼ Put the full strain on the working end to fully tighten and prepare it for use. Make sure that most of the turns are locked to the left under the diagonal turn.

PRUSIK KNOT

This knot was created for climbers by Dr. Carl Prusik in 1931. It binds a *sling* to a main rope that must be at least twice the diameter. The knot grips the main rope when strain is applied to the tail of the sling, yet it allows the sling to slide when the knot is loosened. A series of Prusik Knots can be used as handholds and footholds for climbing a rope. Always check that the finished knot is secure and will hold under strain, especially in icy or wet conditions.

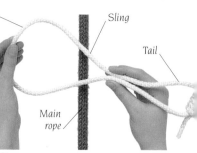

Loop — Sling

Tail

Main rope

❶ **Open** out a *loop* at one end of a sling, and lay the loop on top of the main rope.

Turn

❷ **Pass** the tail of the sling behind the main rope, then through the loop to form the first *turn* around the main rope.

Loop / Tail

❸ **Wind** the tail at least three times around the main rope and through the loop, pulling on the tail to shorten the loop as each turn is made. Apply strain to the tail of the sling to tighten the knot.

Tail

Loop tightens against main rope

BACHMANN KNOT

A *screwgate carabiner* allows this knot to be moved easily along the main rope when it is loosened. When strain is applied to tighten the knot, it should only be applied to the *sling*, and never to the carabiner. The diameter of the sling should be at least half that of the main rope.

Screwgate carabiner

Sling

Main rope

❶ Clip a screwgate carabiner onto a sling. Lay the sling on top of the main rope, and hold the long side of the carabiner against the main rope.

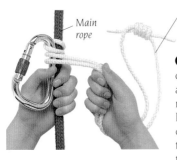

Main rope

Tail

❷ Wind the tail of the sling around the main rope and the long side of the carabiner to bind them loosely together.

Carabiner

Tail

❸ Continue binding the carabiner to the main rope along the long side. Bring the tail through the carabiner to the front of the knot. Apply strain to the tail of the sling to tighten the knot.

Tail

❹ To slide the knot along the main rope, release the strain on the tail of the sling, and use the carabiner to move the knot.

KLEMHEIST KNOT

The second rope used in this variation of the Prusik Knot (p. 104) must be at least half the diameter of the main rope. Soft tubular *tape* may be used instead, since it provides a better grip. Make sure that the *turns* lay snug and even, and test the knot before it is used to take strain.

❶ Pass a *sling* behind the main rope. Working upward, start to wrap the sling around the main rope, leaving a loose tail.

Main rope

Sling

Tail

❷ Continue to wrap the sling tightly and evenly around and up the main rope until a small *loop* is left at the end of the sling. Hold the loop against the front of the main rope. Pick up the loose tail of the sling.

Loop

Tail

Loop

Tail

❸ Pass the tail of the sling up through the loop held against the main rope.

Turns tighten around main rope

Tail

❹ To lock the knot in position, apply a downward strain to the tail of the sling.

ITALIAN HITCH

Climbers use this sliding hitch because it will absorb the energy and control the distance of a fall. The Italian Hitch can also be used for rappelling.

❶ Make a pair of *crossing turns*, laying the right strand of each crossing turn on top of the left strand.

Crossing turn

Left strand

Right strand

Left crossing turn

Right crossing turn

❷ Fold the left crossing turn over to lie on top of the right crossing turn.

❸ Slide the left then the right crossing turn onto a *screwgate carabiner*.

Screwgate carabiner

Right crossing turn

Left crossing turn

Loaded rope

Braking rope

❹ Apply strain to the left (*loaded*) rope to cause the knot to slip. Control the amount and speed of slip by pulling on the right (*braking*) rope.

REVERSED ITALIAN HITCH

Reverse the Italian Hitch by taking strain off the *loaded* rope and applying it to the *braking rope*. The former braking rope becomes the loaded rope, and the former loaded rope becomes the braking rope.

Double
Overhand Loop, p. 116

Bowline with Two
Turns,
p. 113

Bowline on the
Bight, p. 118

Bowline,
p. 112

Double
Fisherman's
Loop, p. 124

Jury Mast
Knot, p. 131

Cargo Net
Knot, p. 130

Bimini Twist, p. 126

Threaded Figure-Eight Loop, p. 115

LOOPS

A loop may be dropped loosely over an object to fix a rope in place, it may be tied around the waist or wrist, or it may be threaded through a ring or an eye of a hook. Loops can also be linked together to join two ropes that are substantially different in size. A few knots in this family form multiple loops at the end of a rope; others create a loop in the middle of a rope. Some loops are fixed in place, while others are designed to slip and change size.

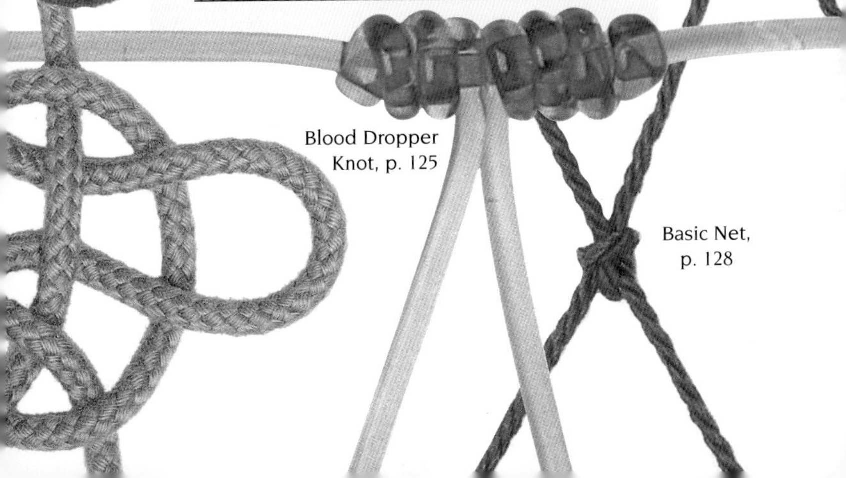

Fisherman's Loop, p. 124

Blood Dropper Knot, p. 125

Basic Net, p. 128

Spanish
Bowline,
p. 120

Single Figure-Eight on the Bight, p. 123

Angler's Loop, p. 122

Figure-Eight
Loop, p. 114

Double
Overhand
Sliding
Loop, p. 117

Portuguese
Bowline,
p. 119

Bowline with
Stopper,
p. 113

ALPINE BUTTERFLY

The Alpine Butterfly can be tied quickly in the middle of a rope. It is a useful knot for securing one climber between two others, since strain can be applied on either side of the knot.

❶ Coil (p. 18) a rope to make two and a half large *turns*.

Half turn

Outer left strand

Outer left strand

❷ Bring the bottom of the outer left strand across and into the center of the remaining two strands.

❸ Pick up the strand that is now on the outer left side of the coil.

Outer left strand

❹ Pass this outer left strand over the other two strands, then through the center of the coil.

❺ Pull the strand through to form a *loop*. Push the remaining strands toward the loop, and work the knot into shape (p. 24).

Loop

Standing part

❻ Pull on both *standing parts* to tighten the knot.

Standing part

111

BOWLINE

The Bowline is a widely used, all-purpose loop that can be tied quickly using one of two methods. The first method (below) is used if the *standing part* is free to lead toward the body as the knot is tied. The second method (opposite) is useful for tying the knot around the waist and for rope that is fixed at one end.

Crossing turn

Working end

Standing part

❶ Take a long *working end* of a rope over its *standing part* to form a *crossing turn*. Hold the crossing turn in place with one hand.

❷ Pass the working end through the crossing turn from back to front. Leave a large *loop* in the working end to form the final loop of the knot.

Loop

Crossing turn

❸ Take the working end behind the standing part.

Working end

Working end

Crossing turn

Working end

Standing part

Standing part

❹ Pass the working end up through the crossing turn from front to back. Pull on the standing part and on the doubled working end to tighten the knot.

BOWLINE – SECOND METHOD

Before tying a Bowline using this method, make sure that the *standing part* leads away from the body. This method can also be used to secure a loose end of a rope to a fixed length, using the fixed length as the standing part.

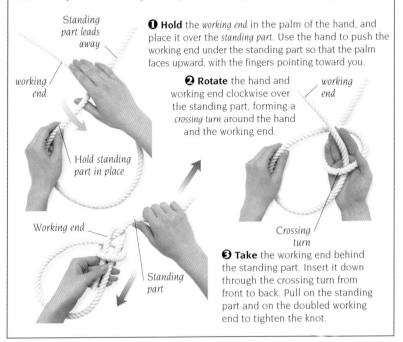

Standing part leads away

working end

Hold standing part in place

Working end

Standing part

❶ **Hold** the *working end* in the palm of the hand, and place it over the *standing part*. Use the hand to push the working end under the standing part so that the palm faces upward, with the fingers pointing toward you.

❷ **Rotate** the hand and working end clockwise over the standing part, forming a *crossing turn* around the hand and the working end.

working end

Crossing turn

❸ **Take** the working end behind the standing part. Insert it down through the crossing turn from front to back. Pull on the standing part and on the doubled working end to tighten the knot.

BOWLINE WITH STOPPER

For extra security, tie knot against Bowline

The addition of an Overhand Knot (p. 28) to the Bowline (opposite), tied with the *working end* taken around the *loop* and tucked under itself, gives a more secure version of the Bowline.

BOWLINE WITH TWO TURNS

A Bowline with Two Turns will prevent a slippery *line* or rope from working loose. Tie a Bowline (opposite), making a second *crossing turn* on top of the first at Step 1.

FIGURE-EIGHT LOOP

Also known as the Double Figure-Eight, this loop is favored by climbers because its distinctive shape makes it easy to check. While it is not as easy to untie as the Bowline (p. 112), it is less likely to be tied incorrectly. The Figure-Eight Loop is formed in the same way as the Figure-Eight (p. 30) using a *bight* rather than the end of a rope.

Crossing turn

Bight

Standing parts

❶ **Double** a length of rope to form a *bight*. Make a *crossing turn*, taking the bight over and behind the *standing parts*.

Eye

Bight

❷ **Bring** the bight to the front of the knot, keeping the *eye* of the turn open.

Bight is used as loop of knot

Crossing turn

Figure-Eight

❸ **Insert** the bight through the crossing turn to form the Figure-Eight. Pull tight. Open out the bight to form the *loop* of the knot.

THREADED FIGURE-EIGHT LOOP

To tie a Figure-Eight Loop through or around an object, such as a ring or pole, use the threaded method. Take care to double the rope neatly so that the finished knot lies snug and even.

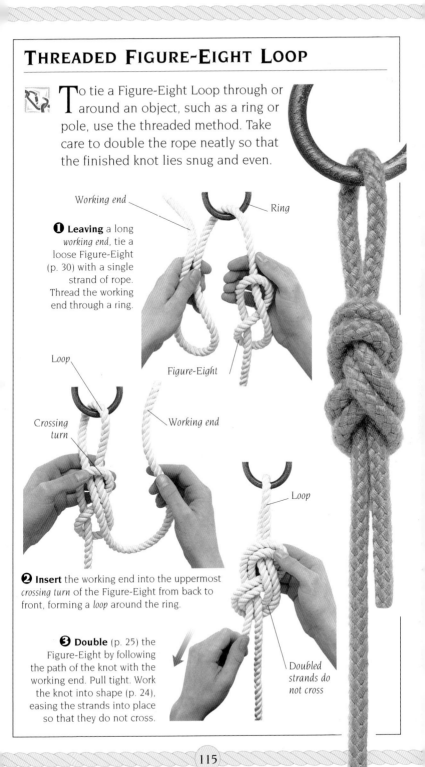

❶ Leaving a long *working end*, tie a loose Figure-Eight (p. 30) with a single strand of rope. Thread the working end through a ring.

Working end

Ring

Figure-Eight

Loop

Crossing turn

Working end

Loop

❷ Insert the working end into the uppermost *crossing turn* of the Figure-Eight from back to front, forming a *loop* around the ring.

❸ Double (p. 25) the Figure-Eight by following the path of the knot with the working end. Pull tight. Work the knot into shape (p. 24), easing the strands into place so that they do not cross.

Doubled strands do not cross

DOUBLE OVERHAND LOOP

The Double Overhand Loop is formed from a double length of rope and is tied in the same manner as a Double Overhand Knot (p. 29). It works well in nylon *line* and produces a neat knot when tied in *thin line*. It is a difficult knot to untie.

Overhand Knot

Bight

Eye of Overhand KnotEye

❶ **Double** a length of rope to form a *bight* at one end. Tie an Overhand Knot (p. 28) near the bight, leaving a large *eye* in the center of the knot.

Overhand Knot

Bight

Eye

Lower double strands

❷ **Take** the bight back over the Overhand Knot, and pass it through the eye of the knot a second time. Pull the bight through.

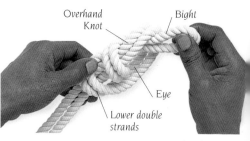

❸ **Pull** on the bight to tighten the knot. At the same time, push the lower double strands over the center double strands into the middle of the knot.

Center double strands

Lower double strands

DOUBLE OVERHAND SLIDING LOOP

This sliding loop is ideal for attaching a fishing *line* to a hook or swivel. It is also very useful for attaching a length of cord to a pair of eyeglasses. Work the knot into a neat shape (p. 24) to make sure that it slides tight smoothly.

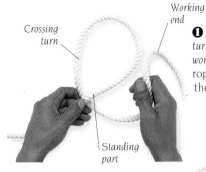

❶ Make a *crossing turn*, passing the *working end* of a rope behind the *standing part*.

Working end

Crossing turn

Standing part

❷ Take the working end around the crossing turn to complete one *turn*, then begin a second.

Crossing turn

Start of second turn

First turn

Second turn

Working end

❸ Complete the second turn around the crossing turn with the working end. Insert the working end through the two turns.

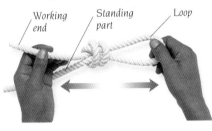

Working end

Standing part

Loop

❹ To tighten the knot, pull on the working end and on the *loop*. Pull on the standing part and on the lower strand of the loop to adjust its size.

BOWLINE
ON THE BIGHT

This double loop can be tied in the middle of a length of rope. The two strands of the loop can then be used separately. If only one strand of the rope is used to take strain, tie the loose strand to the first strand using an Overhand Knot (p. 28).

❶ Double a length of rope to form a *bight*. Make a *crossing turn* by taking the bight over the *standing parts*. Pass the bight through the crossing turn from back to front.

Standing parts

Crossing turn

Bight

❷ Leaving a double-stranded *loop*, open out the bight, and pull it down to extend just below the loop.

Bight

Loop

Standing parts

Bight

Crossing turn

❸ Pass the bight over, then behind the loop and crossing turn. Bring it up behind the standing parts.

❹ To tighten the knot, pull on the standing parts and on the strands of the loop below the crossing turn.

Standing parts

Strands of loop

Crossing turn

PORTUGUESE BOWLINE

By adding an additional *loop* to the Bowline (p. 112), a pair of loops can be made that are adjustable in proportion to each other. Equal strain needs to be taken on both loops to prevent them from changing size while they are being used.

Crossing turn

Standing part

Working end

Second loop

Lower loop

❶ Leaving a long *working end*, take the rope over the *standing part* to make a *crossing turn*. Bring the working end up through the crossing turn from back to front, forming a lower *loop*. Bring the working end back up to form a second loop.

Standing part

Working end

❷ Pass the working end up through the crossing turn from back to front a second time, then take it behind the standing part.

Crossing turn

Working end

❸ Take the working end down through the crossing turn.

Crossing turn

Standing part

Second loop

❹ Tighten the knot by pulling on the standing part with one hand, and on the working end and the second loop with the other.

Working end

SPANISH BOWLINE

A variation of the Bowline (p. 112), the Spanish Bowline has two *loops* that can be adjusted and will lock into position. Strain should be taken equally on both loops. If only one *standing part* of the rope will be used, tie the spare standing part to the first, following Steps 1–3 of the Bowline – Second Method (p. 113).

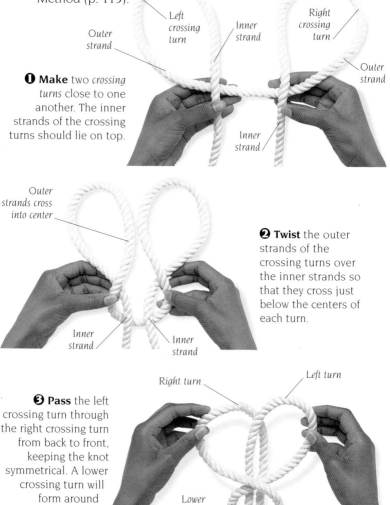

Left crossing turn

Inner strand

Right crossing turn

Outer strand

Outer strand

❶ Make two *crossing turns* close to one another. The inner strands of the crossing turns should lie on top.

Inner strand

Outer strands cross into center

❷ Twist the outer strands of the crossing turns over the inner strands so that they cross just below the centers of each turn.

Inner strand

Inner strand

Right turn

Left turn

❸ Pass the left crossing turn through the right crossing turn from back to front, keeping the knot symmetrical. A lower crossing turn will form around the *standing parts* at the bottom of the knot.

Lower crossing turn

Standing parts

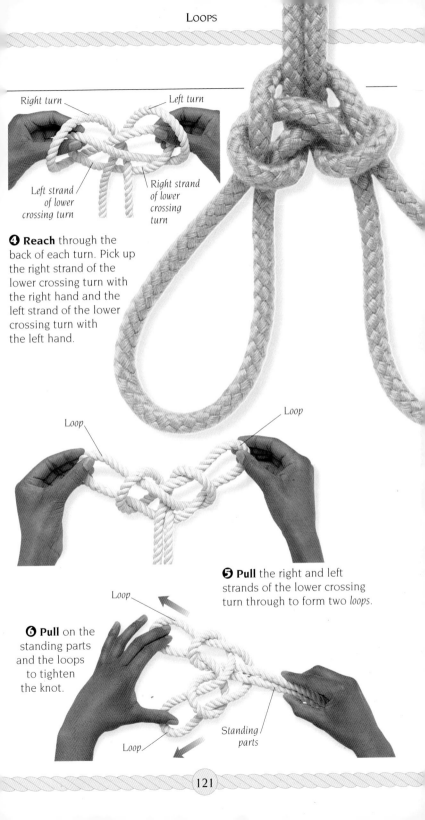

Right turn   Left turn

Left strand
of lower
crossing turn

Right strand
of lower
crossing
turn

❹ Reach through the
back of each turn. Pick up
the right strand of the
lower crossing turn with
the right hand and the
left strand of the lower
crossing turn with
the left hand.

Loop

Loop

❺ Pull the right and left
strands of the lower crossing
turn through to form two *loops*.

Loop

❻ Pull on the
standing parts
and the loops
to tighten
the knot.

Standing
parts

Loop

ANGLER'S LOOP

Often tied in fishing *line*, the Angler's Loop is suitable for all types of *thin line* as well as rope. It is not suitable for use in *large-diameter rope*, since it can be difficult to untie. This is the best knot to use for a permanent *loop* in *shock cord*, when it should be pulled as tight as possible before use.

❶ Make a *crossing turn* toward the end of a rope, taking the *working end* behind the *standing part*

Standing part

Crossing turn

Working end

Working end

❷ Wrap the working end around the crossing turn from front to back to make one and a half *turns*.

Full turn

Half turn

Full turn

Half turn

Crossing turn

❸ Insert the forefinger and thumb through the back of the crossing turn, and bring the full turn over the half turn.

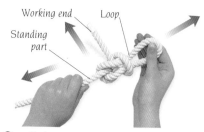

Working end   *Loop*

Standing part

❹ Pull the full turn through the crossing turn to form the *loop* of the knot. Tighten the knot by pulling on the loop, the standing part, and the working end.

USING SHOCK CORD

If *shock cord*, which has a lot of stretch, is used to tie the Angler's Loop, tighten the knot a little at a time; otherwise, it may collapse. Shock cord should be used to tie this knot only if the loop is intended to be permanent, since it is very difficult to untie.

SINGLE FIGURE-EIGHT ON THE BIGHT

This *loop* knot, sometimes known as a Single Bowline on the Bight, is ideal when a loop is needed on a *bight* to take a pull in one direction only. For ease of untying, make sure that the knot is worked neatly into the figure-eight form.

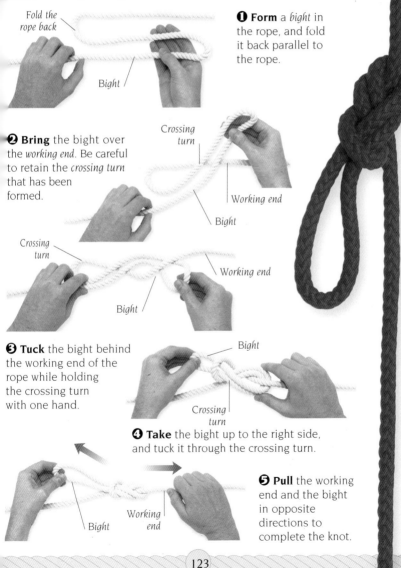

Fold the rope back

Bight

❶ Form a *bight* in the rope, and fold it back parallel to the rope.

❷ Bring the bight over the *working end*. Be careful to retain the *crossing turn* that has been formed.

Crossing turn

Working end

Bight

Crossing turn

Working end

Bight

❸ Tuck the bight behind the working end of the rope while holding the crossing turn with one hand.

Bight

Crossing turn

❹ Take the bight up to the right side, and tuck it through the crossing turn.

Bight

Working end

❺ Pull the working end and the bight in opposite directions to complete the knot.

FISHERMAN'S LOOP

Similar to the Fisherman's Knot (p. 74), the Fisherman's Loop uses two Overhand Knots (p. 28) to form a fixed *loop*. The drawing together of two knots to form one gives this knot a symbolic romantic value.

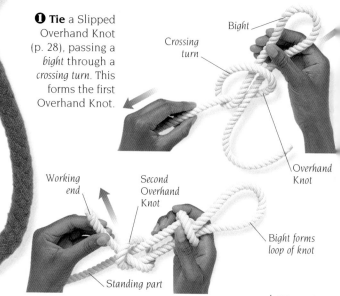

❶ **Tie** a Slipped Overhand Knot (p. 28), passing a *bight* through a *crossing turn*. This forms the first Overhand Knot.

Bight

Crossing turn

Overhand Knot

Working end

Second Overhand Knot

Bight forms loop of knot

Standing part

❷ **To** tie the second Overhand Knot, take the *working end* over the *standing part* and around itself. Tuck the working end under itself, then pull on it to tighten the second Overhand Knot.

Loop

Working end

Standing part

❸ **To** complete the Fisherman's Loop, pull on the standing part and on the *loop* so that the two Overhand Knots slide together.

DOUBLE FISHERMAN'S LOOP

For extra security when using slippery rope, double (p. 25) each Overhand Knot as it is made while tying the Fisherman's Loop (above).

BLOOD DROPPER KNOT

This knot is tied at the end of fishing *line* to form a *loop* to which a short length of line with a fly or a baited hook can be fixed. The twists in this knot identify it as a member of the *blood knot* family.

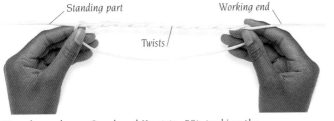

Standing part

Working end

Twists

❶ Tie a large, loose Overhand Knot (p. 28), tucking the *working end* over and under the *standing part*. Tuck the working end five times around the standing part, forming ten twists.

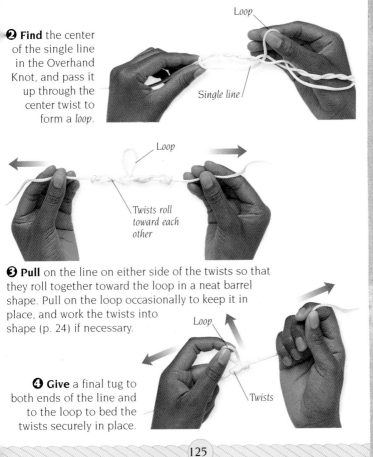

❷ Find the center of the single line in the Overhand Knot, and pass it up through the center twist to form a *loop*.

Loop

Single line

Loop

Twists roll toward each other

❸ Pull on the line on either side of the twists so that they roll together toward the loop in a neat barrel shape. Pull on the loop occasionally to keep it in place, and work the twists into shape (p. 24) if necessary.

Loop

❹ Give a final tug to both ends of the line and to the loop to bed the twists securely in place.

Twists

BIMINI TWIST

The Bimini Twist is used to form a long *loop* at the end of a braided or monofilament fishing *line*. Originally developed for big-game fishing, it now has a place in all types of fishing. The technique used to tie this knot needs two pairs of hands, and may take some practice.

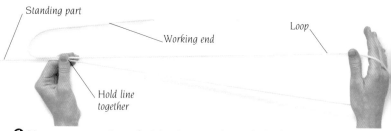

Standing part

Working end

Loop

Hold line together

❶ Measure approximately 5 ft (1½ m) at the end of a line, and fold it back to form a *loop*. Hold the line together with one hand, leaving a *working end* of about 18 in (45 cm). Open out the end of the loop with the other hand.

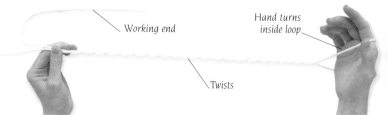

Working end

Hand turns inside loop

Twists

❷ Keeping the line under tension, twist the hand inside and around the end of the loop, forming twists in the two lines of the loop. Continue until approximately 20 twists have been made in the lines.

❸ Maintaining the tension in the line, ask an assistant to take the remainder of the loop in both hands. Hold the *standing part* of the line with one hand and the working end in the other. The assistant should now open out the loop with both hands to force the twists toward the standing part and the working end.

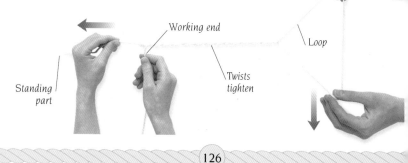

Working end

Loop

Standing part

Twists tighten

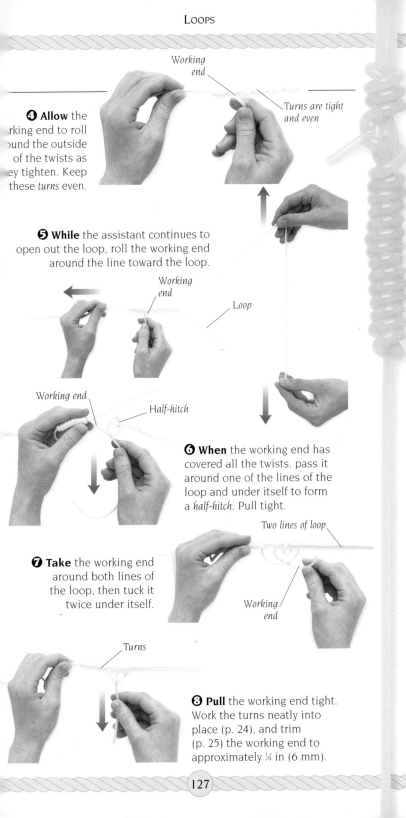

Working end

Turns are tight and even

❹ **Allow** the working end to roll around the outside of the twists as they tighten. Keep these *turns* even.

❺ **While** the assistant continues to open out the loop, roll the working end around the line toward the loop.

Working end

Loop

Working end

Half-hitch

❻ **When** the working end has covered all the twists, pass it around one of the lines of the loop and under itself to form a *half-hitch*. Pull tight.

Two lines of loop

❼ **Take** the working end around both lines of the loop, then tuck it twice under itself.

Working end

Turns

❽ **Pull** the working end tight. Work the turns neatly into place (p. 24), and trim (p. 25) the working end to approximately ¼ in (6 mm).

BASIC NET-MAKING

A net is a series of holes with a line knotted around them. The line to make these knots is carried on a *netting needle*. A wooden dowel may be used as a gauge to ensure that the meshes of the net are of a similar size. The oldest knot was found in a 9,000-year-old piece of netting on the Karelian Isthmus – that knot was the Sheet Bend (p. 68) used here.

❶ **Make** a row of *loops* along a bar with Cow Hitches (p. 86) or Clove Hitches (p. 56). Working from left to right, bring the needle down, over, and behind the gauge, and up through the first top loop.

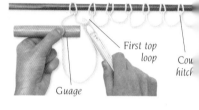

First top loop

Cow hitch

Guage

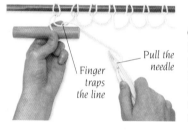

Pull the needle

Finger traps the line

❷ **Pull** the needle to bring the gauge tight to the top loop. With your left index finger, trap the line on the gauge as it comes up through the top loop.

LOADING A NEEDLE

To carry the large quantity of line required to make a Basic Net, use a *netting needle* made of either wood, plastic or metal. Load the needle by using the following steps.

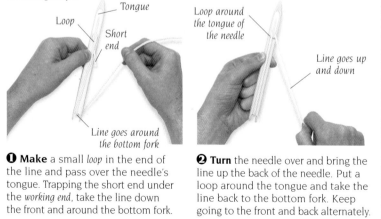

Tongue

Loop

Short end

Line goes around the bottom fork

Loop around the tongue of the needle

Line goes up and down

❶ **Make** a small *loop* in the end of the line and pass over the needle's tongue. Trapping the short end under the *working end*, take the line down the front and around the bottom fork.

❷ **Turn** the needle over and bring the line up the back of the needle. Put a loop around the tongue and take the line back to the bottom fork. Keep going to the front and back alternately.

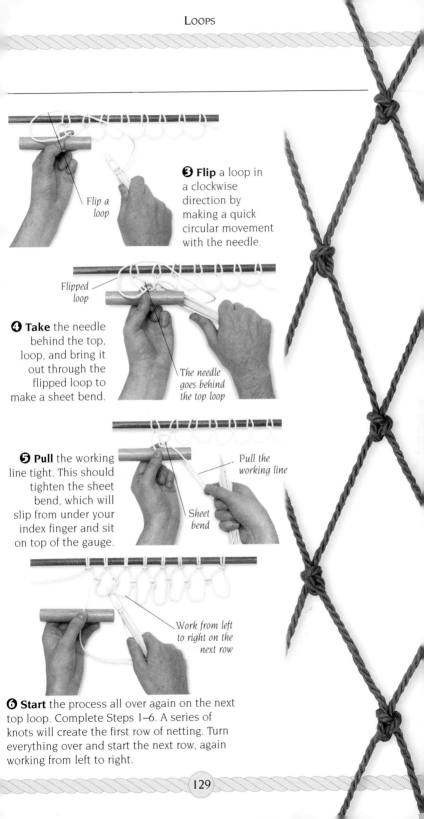

❸ Flip a loop in a clockwise direction by making a quick circular movement with the needle.

Flip a loop

Flipped loop

❹ Take the needle behind the top, loop, and bring it out through the flipped loop to make a sheet bend.

The needle goes behind the top loop

❺ Pull the working line tight. This should tighten the sheet bend, which will slip from under your index finger and sit on top of the gauge.

Pull the working line

Sheet bend

Work from left to right on the next row

❻ Start the process all over again on the next top loop. Complete Steps 1–6. A series of knots will create the first row of netting. Turn everything over and start the next row, again working from left to right.

CARGO NET KNOT

Heavy rope used to make cargo nets cannot be netted in the basic sheet bend method. Use the following knot for such ropes. Arrange the ropes at a 90-degree angle to one another, and use the shorter horizontal rope to make the tuck.

Longer rope

Short rope

❶ Place the short working rope under the longer rope.

❷ Hold the long rope above and below the short rope, and make a *crossing turn*. Pass the short rope through the crossing turn.

Crossing turn

Short rope passes through the crossing turn

Working end

Crossing turn

❸ Bring the *working end* of the short rope over the crossing turn. Then pass it through the crossing turn again.

❹ Pull tight vertically, then horizontally to work the knot into shape (p. 24).

130

JURY MAST KNOT

This decorative knot, formed from three *crossing turns*, can be used to provide the multiple *loops* needed to secure the *rigging* of a boat in an emergency. It is said that cannon balls used to be carried in this knot.

Left crossing turn

❶ Pass a rope behind itself to form three large, loose *crossing turns*, each one overlapping the previous turn.

Right crossing turn lies on top of center turn

Center turn lies on top of left turn

Right inner strand

❷ Insert the right hand through the front of the right crossing turn and under the center turn. Take hold of the inner strand of the left turn. Insert the left hand under the left crossing turn and over the center turn. Take hold of the inner strand of the right turn.

Center turn

Left inner strand

Side loop

Side loop

❸ Pull the inner strands through the outer crossing turns to form two *loops* at the sides of the knot.

Side loop

Upper loop

Side loop

❹ Pull on the side loops, and pull on the top of the center turn to form an upper loop. Adjust the three loops to form a symmetrical knot.

Five-Strand Sennit, p. 134

Four-Strand Sennit, p. 135

Six-Strand Sennit, p. 13

Ocean-Plait Mat, p. 136

Three-Strand Plait, p. 134

Oval Mat, p. 138

Eight-Strand Square Sennit, p. 145

BRAIDS & SENNITS

A braid is made up of a number of strands of rope interwoven in a simple, repetitive pattern. Strands woven in complex patterns are known as sennits. Most braids and sennits will create a stronger length of rope that is compact and flexible; some will create a flat knot. Braids and sennits must be woven with an even tension to produce knots that are neat and decorative.

Round Crown Sennit, p. 142

THREE-STRAND BRAID

This is the simplest form of *braid*. Often used to dress hair, it shows the basic principle of braiding, in which alternate outer strands are brought into the center of a knot. This braid can also be made with six strands, woven together in three pairs of two strands.

Outer strand

Center strand

❶ **Bind** three strands of rope together at one end. Keeping tension on all strands, take one outer strand over the center strand.

Outer strand

Center strand

❷ **Take** the outer strand on the other side of the braid over the new center strand into the middle of the knot.

Braid

❸ **Continue** taking alternate outer strands into the middle of the knot. *Seize* (p. 25) the three strand ends together when the braid is complete.

FIVE-STRAND SENNIT

Made with five strands of rope bound at one end, this knot follows the same principle as the Three-Strand Braid (above).

Outer strand crosses to center of knot

❶ **Holding** the strands in both hands to maintain an even tension, take alternate outer strands over two strands into the middle of the knot. *Seize* (p. 25) the strands together when the sennit is complete.

FOUR-STRAND SENNIT

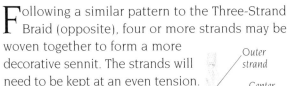

Following a similar pattern to the Three-Strand Braid (opposite), four or more strands may be woven together to form a more decorative sennit. The strands will need to be kept at an even tension.

Outer strand

Center strands

Opposite outer strand

❶ **With** four strands bound together at one end, take one outer strand over the two center strands to place it beside the opposite outer strand.

Outer strand

Single strand

❷ **Take** the opposite outer strand over a single strand toward the middle of the knot.

Outer strand

❸ **Continue** taking the outer strand on one side of the braid over two strands, and the opposite outer strand over one strand. When the sennit is complete, *seize* (p. 25) the strands together.

SIX-STRAND SENNIT

A broad, almost symmetrical sennit, this knot needs to be kept flat and held under tension while being tied.

❶ **Starting** with six strands bound at one end and laid side by side, take alternate outer strands over three strands on one side of the knot and over two strands on the opposite side of the knot. *Seize* (p. 25) the strands together.

Outer strands

OCEAN-BRAID MAT

This flat, decorative knot is based on a simple Overhand Knot (p. 28). Since a lot of rope is needed to complete the mat, it is essential to begin by generously estimating (p. 22) the length of rope required. Large mats may need to be quadrupled, depending on the thickness of the rope.

❶ Tie a loose Overhand Knot toward the right end of the rope, leaving enough rope on the short end to complete Steps 2–5. Hold the knot so that the large *loop* is at the top, with two lower, smaller *eyes* on either side of the crossed rope.

Upper loop

Eye

Left lower loop

Right lower loop

❷ Pull on the crossed strands of the Overhand Knot to form two lower loops, each one approximately three-quarters of the length of the finished mat.

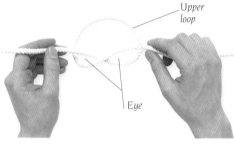

Upper loop

Eye

Eye

Crossed strands

❸ Twist each lower loop over in a clockwise direction. Leave an eye approximately the same size as the upper loop above the crossed strands.

Left lower loop

Right lower loop

❹ Position the right lower loop over the center of the left lower loop. Keep the pattern of eyes and crossed strands even.

Right rope

❺ Take the right length of loose rope over the right lower loop, under both strands of the left lower loop, and over the tip of the right lower loop.

Right lower loop

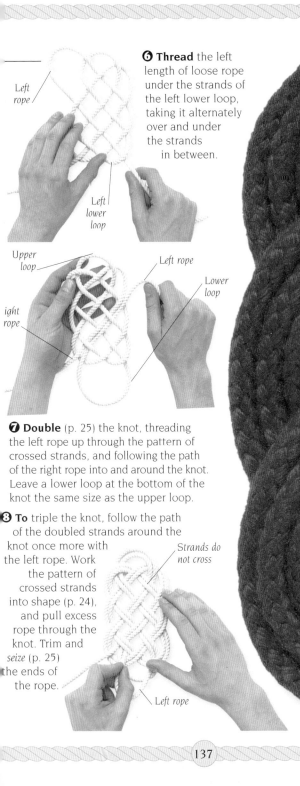

⑥ Thread the left length of loose rope under the strands of the left lower loop, taking it alternately over and under the strands in between.

Left rope

Left lower loop

Upper loop

Left rope

Lower loop

Right rope

⑦ Double (p. 25) the knot, threading the left rope up through the pattern of crossed strands, and following the path of the right rope into and around the knot. Leave a lower loop at the bottom of the knot the same size as the upper loop.

⑧ To triple the knot, follow the path of the doubled strands around the knot once more with the left rope. Work the pattern of crossed strands into shape (p. 24), and pull excess rope through the knot. Trim and *seize* (p. 25) the ends of the rope.

Strands do not cross

Left rope

OVAL MAT

This handsome mat can be created from simple *crossing turns*. Starting in the middle of the rope, make the basic design, then even out the *loops* to obtain a good shape. Then double (p. 25) and triple the rope using both ends of the rope. Make sure you have enough rope (p. 22) to make the mat.

Rope passes over the standing part

❶ Make a series of three crossing turns with a clockwise twist, working from right to left. Make sure the rope lies on top of the *standing part* as the crossing turn is made.

Crossing turns

❷ Push the left turn under the center turn, and take the right turn over the center turn.

Center turn

Left turn passes under the center turn

Right turn passes over the center turn

Left turn

Right turn

❸ Continue to bring the outer turns into the middle. As the left and right turns meet, place the left on top of the right turn.

Loop

❹ Form a loop with the *working end*. Take the working end across the interleaved turns, passing it over, under, over, over, under, and over.

Working end *Standing part*

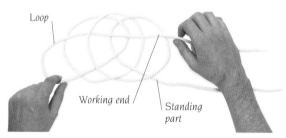

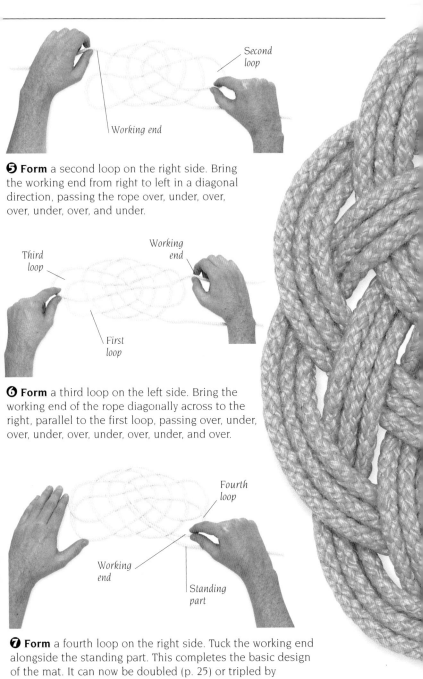

Second loop

Working end

❺ **Form** a second loop on the right side. Bring the working end from right to left in a diagonal direction, passing the rope over, under, over, over, under, over, and under.

Third loop

Working end

First loop

❻ **Form** a third loop on the left side. Bring the working end of the rope diagonally across to the right, parallel to the first loop, passing over, under, over, under, over, under, over, under, and over.

Fourth loop

Working end

Standing part

❼ **Form** a fourth loop on the right side. Tuck the working end alongside the standing part. This completes the basic design of the mat. It can now be doubled (p. 25) or tripled by following the pattern with either end of the rope.

CHAIN SENNIT

The Chain Sennit is a series of interlinked *loops* that can be made in the middle of a length of rope. It needs a lot of rope, and can be used as a temporary *shortening*.

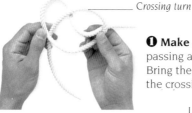

Crossing turn

❶ **Make** a *crossing turn* by passing a rope over itself. Bring the rope behind the crossing turn.

Loop

❷ **Pull** the rope through the crossing turn to form a *loop*. Take the rope behind the loop again.

❸ **Repeat** Step 2 as many times as required until a chain of interlocking loops has formed.

Loop

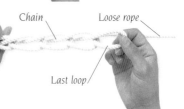

Chain   *Loose rope*

Last loop

❹ **When** the Chain Sennit is long enough, pull the last loop through. If the loose rope is now pulled, the Chain Sennit will undo.

End of rope is pulled through loop

❺ **To** lock the loops of the completed Chain Sennit in place, pull the loose rope through the last loop.

Last loop

SQUARE CHAIN SENNIT

A short length of Square Chain Sennit can make a fine decoration in a lanyard; a longer piece will make a good handhold on a dog leash or a jump rope. By starting as the Chain Sennit (opposite), but then creating a second *loop* to work with, it is possible to create this Sennit with just one strand.

❶ **Make** a *loop* by completing Steps 1–2 of the Chain Sennit (opposite). Make a second loop with the *working end*, and put this through the first loop.

First loop

Second loop

Working end

❷ **Pull** the second loop through the first loop, leaving an extra working loop or ear.

Ear

Second loop

Working end

Loop

Ear

❸ **Using** the working end, *tuck* a loop through the ear.

Loop passes through the ear

Square Knot with two ears

❹ **Hold** the loop formed in Step 3 with one hand, and tuck another loop through the ear. By pulling this loop tight, the knot will tighten up into a square form, leaving two ears for forming the chain (see inset).

❺ **Repeat** the tucking of a loop and the tightening of a loop using alternate ears. To lock the chain, pull the working end through the first loop and then through the second loop.

First loop

Second loop

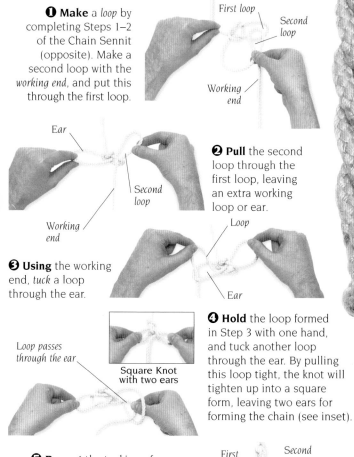

ROUND CROWN SENNIT

A series of Crown Knots (p. 36) made on top of one another creates this attractive sennit. Tying all the knots in the same direction will create a Round Crown Sennit (finished knot, far right); tying them in alternate directions will form a Square Crown Sennit (right). Before starting a Round Crown Sennit, bind four strands of rope together at one end with a knot or *seizing* (p. 168).

Second strand

First strand

Bight

❶ Pick up a first strand, and pass it in a counterclockwise direction over the second strand. Leave a *bight* between these first two strands.

Bight

Second strand

Fourth strand

Third strand

❸ Pass the third strand over the second and fourth strands. Pick up the fourth strand, and pass it over the third strand, then down through the bight formed between the first and second strands. This forms a four-strand Crown Knot.

Third strand

Second strand

First strand

❷ Working in the same direction, take the second strand, and pass it over the first and third strands.

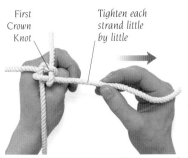

First Crown Knot

Tighten each strand little by little

❹ Tighten the knot by pulling on each strand in turn, working around the knot in two or three cycles so that the Crown Knot lies snug and even.

❺ Repeat Steps 1–4 to make a series of Crown Knots in the same direction, pulling each one tight on top of the previous knot to form a Round Crown Sennit.

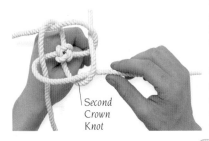

Second Crown Knot

SQUARE CROWN SENNIT

Start a Square Crown Sennit by binding together four strands of rope with a knot or *seizing* (p. 168).

First Crown Knot

Second Crown Knot is tied in clockwise direction

❶ **Tie** a four-strand Crown Knot, following Steps 1–4 of the Round Crown Sennit (opposite). Working in the opposite (clockwise) direction, tie a second Crown Knot on top of the first.

Third Crown Knot is tied in counter-clockwise direction

❷ **Pulling** each one tight, continue to tie a series of Crown Knots in alternate directions to form a Square Crown Sennit.

SIX-STRAND ROUND CROWN SENNIT

To form a cylindrical tube from a sennit, tie a series of Crown Knots with six or more strands of rope fixed at one end. Tie the knots in the same direction and in the same way as the Round Crown Sennit (opposite). Use the tube as a decorative covering for a *core*, such as another rope.

FOUR-STRAND ROUND SENNIT

Four strands of rope can be used to make a sennit that appears round. The sennit can be enhanced by using different-colored strands to create decorative patterns. If four pairs of strands are used, a *braid* similar to multibraided rope (p. 11) can be achieved. Make the sennit without interruption to maintain a neat pattern.

Outer strand

Outer strand

❶ Lay four strands of rope fixed at one end side by side. Pick up one of the outer strands, and take it behind the two center strands.

Outer strand

❷ Bring this outer strand to the front of the knot, and place it between the two center strands.

Outer strand

❸ Pick up the outer strand on the opposite side, and take it behind the two strands in the center of the knot.

❹ Take this outer strand to the front of the knot and between the two center strands.

Outer strands

❺ Continue this pattern, taking alternate, new outer strands behind then into the middle of the strands in the center. Keep an even tension as the knot is worked. Secure the sennit by *seizing* the ends (p. 25).

EIGHT-STRAND SQUARE SENNIT

Although this sennit uses eight strands, it is created by repeating a four-step process – two steps bringing the strands to the front and two steps taking them to the back. If you stop during the making of this sennit, it is important to restart in the correct sequence. Stop with three strands in one hand and five in the other.

Outer left strand

Hold three strands in the right hand

❶ Start with three strands flat in the right hand and five strands flat in the left hand. Then bring the outer strand on the left over the front to the middle of the sennit. Hold it in the right hand.

Outer right strand

❷ Bring the outer strand on the right over the front to the middle. Then hold it in the left hand.

Outer left strand passes behind the sennit

❸ Take what is now the outer strand on the left behind the sennit to the middle. Hold it in the right hand.

Outer right strand passes behind the sennit

❹ Take what is now the outer strand on the right behind the sennit to the middle. Hold it in the left hand.

Sennit develops as Steps 1–4 are repeated

❺ Repeat Steps 1–4 to form the sennit. *Seize* (p. 25) the ends of the strands.

Long Splice, p. 140

Eye Splice, p. 137

Common Whipping, p. 160

Right-Angle Splice, p. 156

Short Splice, p. 138

Palm & Needle Whipping I, p. 148

French Whipping, p. 145

SPLICES & WHIPPINGS

A splice is used to join two lengths of rope of equal diameter, to make a loop at the end of a rope, or to bind the end of a rope. Splices are strong, and once completed are permanent. A whipping binds the end of a rope to prevent the strands from coming undone. Whipping turns must be pulled tight as they are made to prevent them from working loose.

BACK SPLICE

This splice gives a permanent finish to the end of a *three-strand rope* to prevent it from unlaying. Tape (p. 16) the strand ends so that they tuck easily under the *laid strands*. If the rope is stiff, use a *Swedish fid* to separate the strands (see opposite). A Back Splice will increase the diameter of a rope by one-third.

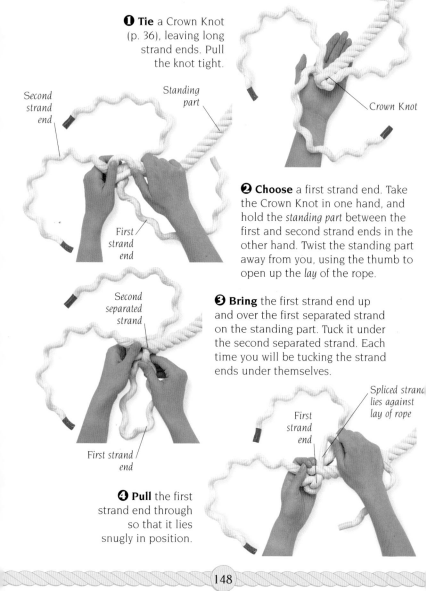

❶ Tie a Crown Knot (p. 36), leaving long strand ends. Pull the knot tight.

Second strand end

Standing part

Crown Knot

First strand end

❷ Choose a first strand end. Take the Crown Knot in one hand, and hold the *standing part* between the first and second strand ends in the other hand. Twist the standing part away from you, using the thumb to open up the *lay* of the rope.

Second separated strand

❸ Bring the first strand end up and over the first separated strand on the standing part. Tuck it under the second separated strand. Each time you will be tucking the strand ends under themselves.

First strand end

Spliced strand lies against lay of rope

First strand end

❹ Pull the first strand end through so that it lies snugly in position.

First strand end

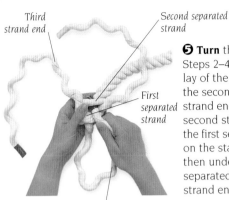

Third strand end

Second separated strand

First separated strand

Second strand end

⑤ Turn the rope. Repeat Steps 2–4, opening up the lay of the rope between the second and third strand ends. Tuck the second strand end over the first separated strand on the standing part, then under the second separated strand. Pull the strand end through.

⑥ Open up the lay of the rope between the third and first strand ends as before. Tuck the third strand end over and under the separated strands. Pull through to complete one full cycle of *tucks*.

Third strand end

Second separated strand

Pull strand ends into position

⑦ Repeat Steps 2–6 to complete two more cycles of tucks with all three strand ends, pulling them snugly into position after each cycle. Trim (p. 25) the strand ends.

USING A FID

If a rope is stiff, it will be difficult to push its strands apart and tuck the strand ends through. Use a *Swedish fid* to separate the strands, keeping the hollow eye of the fid uppermost. Push the strand end through the hollow eye of the fid so that it passes underneath the strand, then pull through.

TAPERING A SPLICE

Spliced *three-strand rope* can be tapered before being
trimmed to give it a neat finish and to keep it from
working loose. Tapering tucks are made in the same
way as splicing tucks (p. 148), with the strand ends
split in half before each cycle of tucks is made.

Tape

❶ Take the strand ends
of a completed splice,
and split each one in half.
Replace the tape at the
end of one-half of each
split strand end.

Halved
strand end

Make tuck
against lay
of rope

Taped strand end

❷ Make tapering tucks
with the three strand ends
by tucking the taped half
of each strand end back into
the rope as for Steps 2–4 of the
Back Splice (p. 148). Leave the
untaped strand ends free.

Halved
strand ends
remain
untucked

❸ Split each tucked
strand end in half again,
taping the end of one
half of each as before.
Make tapering tucks
with the taped strand
ends as for Step 2.

Loose
strand end

❹ Split, tape, and tuck
each taped strand end a
third time. Trim (p. 25) all
the loose strand ends,
leaving a short end on the
last row of strand ends so
that they do not work loose.
Work a tapered splice
into shape by rolling
it underfoot (p. 24).

EYE SPLICE

The Eye Splice forms a permanent *loop* at the end of *three-strand rope*. Three cycles of splicing *tucks* are sufficient for natural rope; five cycles are needed for synthetic rope since it is more slippery.

Standing part

❶ Unlay (p. 23) the end of a length of three-strand rope. Fold the rope back on itself in a counterclockwise direction to form a *loop*, spreading the unlaid strand ends evenly against the *standing part*.

Loop

First strand end

Standing part

❷ Choose the uppermost strand end, and tuck it under the nearest strand on the standing part, tucking against the *lay* of the rope.

Second strand end

Standing part

❸ Turn the standing part, and – still working against the lay of the rope – tuck the second strand end under the next strand.

Third strand end

❹ Turn the standing part, and tuck the third strand end under the strand on the standing part lying between the first two strands. This completes a first cycle of tucks.

Pull strand ends tight against standing part

❺ Follow Steps 2–4 of the Back Splice (p. 148) to make further cycles of splicing tucks. Taper (opposite) or trim (p. 25) the strand ends.

SHORT SPLICE

The Short Splice forms a strong join between two lengths of rope that are the same size and are made of the same material. This splice increases the diameter of a rope, and may not be suitable if the rope is to pass through a *pulley block*. Three full rows of *tucks* on either rope are sufficient for natural ropes; five rows will be needed for synthetic ropes, which are more slippery.

Unlaid strand end

Unlaid strands are interlaced

❶ Unlay (p. 23) the strands at the ends of two lengths of rope. Lay the two ropes end to end, then insert each unlaid strand end between two unlaid strand ends of the second rope.

❷ Pull on each set of unlaid strand ends so that the two ropes are drawn tightly together.

Ropes are married together

Second strand

Unlaid strand end

❸ Pick up an unlaid strand end and, working against the *lay* of the rope, take it over the adjacent strand from the opposite rope, and tuck it under the second strand of the opposite rope.

Adjacent strand

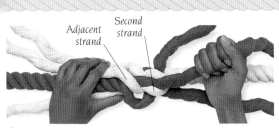

Adjacent strand — Second strand

❹ **Roll** the rope toward you, and repeat Step 3 with the second and third strand ends of the same rope, making sure they are tucked against the lay of the rope.

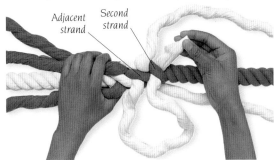

Adjacent strand — Second strand

❺ **Turn** the ropes so that they lie in the opposite direction. Tuck one of the unlaid strands over the adjacent and under the second strand of the opposite rope, still working against the lay of the rope.

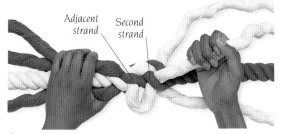

Adjacent strand — Second strand

❻ **Tuck** the remaining two unlaid strand ends into the rope as before. Pull each strand end tight. This completes a full cycle of tucks.

Third cycles of tucks

❼ **Follow** Steps 3–6 to make additional cycles of tucks with the strand ends, always working against the lay of the rope. Trim (p. 25) or taper (p. 150) the strand ends.

LONG SPLICE

The Long Splice is used to join *three-strand rope* when the increase in the rope's diameter needs to be kept to a minimum so that it can be passed through a *pulley block*. This splice is not as strong as a Short Splice (p. 152).

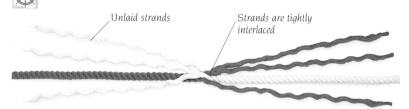

Unlaid strands

Strands are tightly interlaced

❶ Unlay (p. 23) the strands of two ropes to approximately 40 times the diameter of the rope. Lay the two ropes end to end and interlace the unlaid strands by placing each one between two strands of the opposite rope. Pull on each set of strands to marry the ropes together tightly.

❷ Holding the two ropes in place with one hand, unlay a strand in one of the ropes for three or four twists. Replace it with a neighboring strand end from the opposite rope.

Strand is unlaid

Strand end replaces unlaid strand

❸ Continue to unlay the strand and replace it with the strand end from the opposite rope until only a short strand end from the opposite rope remains.

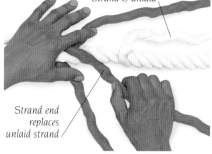

Overhand Knot

Short strand end

Tuck left strand end over and under right strand end

❹ Repeat Steps 1–3 to replace a strand in the opposite rope with a strand end from the first rope. Tie an Overhand Knot (p. 28) with the strand ends in the center and at each end of the splice.

❺ Pull each Overhand Knot tight so that the strand ends bed evenly into the *lay* of the rope.

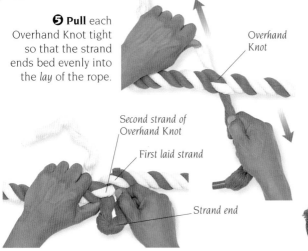

Overhand Knot

Second strand of Overhand Knot

First laid strand

Strand end

❻ At each Overhand Knot, take one strand end and pass it over the second strand of the Overhand Knot. Tuck it under the first laid strand, working against the lay of the rope.

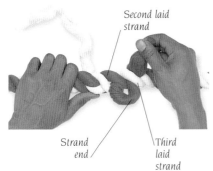

Second laid strand

❼ Take the same strand end and tuck it over, then under the second and third laid strands, still working against the lay of the rope.

Strand end

Third laid strand

❽ Repeat Steps 6–7 with the second strand end of each Overhand Knot. Trim (p. 25) each strand end, leaving a short end.

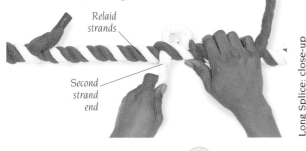

Relaid strands

Second strand end

Long Splice: close-up

Long Splice

RIGHT-ANGLE SPLICE

There are times when you may need to join a rope squarely at right angles, perhaps to the outer rope of a cargo net. This neat splice is perfect for such occasions. The ropes used can be of equal size, or a smaller rope can be spliced to a large rope. It is not advisable to splice a larger rope to a small rope.

Standing rope

Working rope

Tuck the left strand

❶ Unlay (p. 23) the working rope and spread the strands out evenly at right angles to the standing rope. Tuck the left strand under two strands on the standing rope.

Middle strand

❷ Tuck the middle strand under the strand on the standing rope that is on the right side of the tucked left strand. It will come out at the same place as the first strand.

Right strand is tucked alongside middle strand

❸ Tuck the right strand into the standing rope at the same place as the middle strand, but pass it under two strands.

❹ Bring the left strand over the two strands on the standing rope. Tuck it back under the middle strand on the working rope.

Left strand is tucked under middle strand

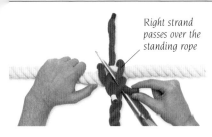

Right strand passes over the standing rope

❺ Bring the right-hand strand over two strands on the standing rope. Tuck it back under the right strand on the working rope.

Middle strand is tucked under the working rope

❻ Turn the whole splice over. Bring the middle strand over two strands on the standing rope, and tuck it back under the top strand of the working rope. The three strands should now exit evenly around the working rope.

Tuck down the working rope

❼ Make a series of tucks down the working rope as in the Eye Splice (p. 151).

First cycle of tucks

Second cycle of tucks

❽ Make a total of three full cycles of tucks for natural rope or five full cycles of tucks for synthetic rope. Taper the splice (p. 150) if required, and trim (p. 25).

GROMMET

The Grommet uses a single strand from a length of *three-strand rope* to make a strong ring. If the two remaining strands are also used to make Grommets, a set of *deck quoits* for playing on board ship can be made.

Right strand

Left strand

❶ **Unlay** (p. 23) a strand of rope approximately three and a half times the circumference of the finished Grommet. Keep as much of the twist as possible in the strand.

Unlaid strand retains twist

Left strand

Right strand

❷ **Lay** the strand out in a ring to the size of the Grommet required. Cross the right strand over the left strand.

Left strand

Groove

Right strand

❸ **Working** in a clockwise direction, relay (p. 23) the left strand around the grooves of the ring. Apply a slight twist to the left strand as it is worked.

Left strand

Right strand

❹ **Continue** relaying the left strand around the ring until it has been relaid past the right strand and into the next groove.

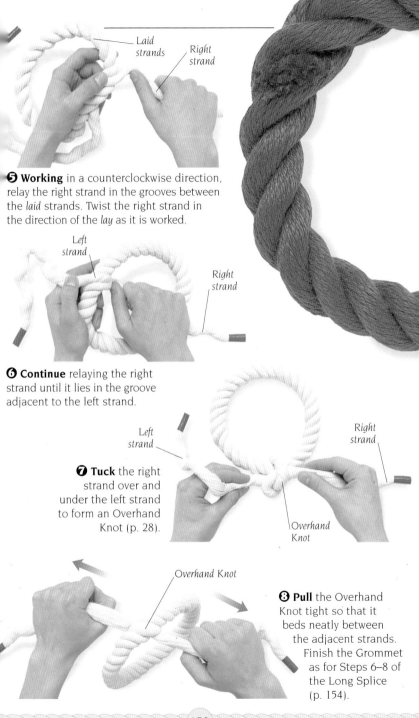

Laid strands — Right strand

❺ Working in a counterclockwise direction, relay the right strand in the grooves between the *laid* strands. Twist the right strand in the direction of the *lay* as it is worked.

Left strand — Right strand

❻ Continue relaying the right strand until it lies in the groove adjacent to the left strand.

Left strand — Right strand

❼ Tuck the right strand over and under the left strand to form an Overhand Knot (p. 28).

Overhand Knot

Overhand Knot

❽ Pull the Overhand Knot tight so that it beds neatly between the adjacent strands. Finish the Grommet as for Steps 6–8 of the Long Splice (p. 154).

COMMON WHIPPING

The simplest of the whippings, the Common Whipping is suitable for both *three-strand* and *braided rope*. It can be used to stop the end of a rope from fraying, or to make a mark at any point on a rope. When finishing, it may be helpful to use a Marlingspike Hitch (p. 88) to pull on the short end so that the *whipping twine* does not cut into the hand.

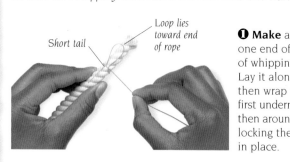

Short tail

Loop lies toward end of rope

❶ Make a loop at one end of a length of whipping twine. Lay it along a rope, then wrap the twine first underneath and then around the rope locking the loop in place.

❷ Working toward the rope end, make a series of *whipping turns* around the rope and loop until the whipping is one and a half times the diameter of the rope. Leave the loop free at the end of the rope.

End of loop

Whipping turns

Loop

❸ Insert the twine into the loop, and pull it through.

Loop is pulled under whipping

❹ To bury the loop inside the turns, pull tightly on the short end left at the beginning of the whipping. Trim (p. 25) the ends as required.

Short tail

FRENCH WHIPPING

The *half-hitches* used here create a very tight whipping, with each *turn* locked off from the one before. The half-hitches are tied in the same direction to create a decorative spiral effect. A French Whipping, or the more elaborate alternative, the Moku Whipping (below), can be made around tool handles for a good grip.

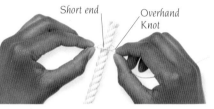

Short end

Overhand Knot

❶ **Tie** an Overhand Knot (p. 28) around a rope with *whipping twine*, leaving a short end.

Short end

Half-hitch

❷ **Make** a half-hitch by taking the whipping twine behind the rope and tucking it underneath itself at the front of the rope. Catch the short end in the hitch as the twine is pulled tight.

❸ **Make** a series of half-hitches in the same way, pulling each one tight until the whipping is one and a half times as long as the diameter of the rope.

MOKU WHIPPING

Begin as for Step 1 of the French Whipping (above), leaving two long ends. Tie *half-hitches* as for Step 2, using alternate ends and taking the second end behind the rope in the opposite direction to the first. Finish each end as in Step 4.

Second tuck secures knot

Final half-hitch

❹ **Finish** by tucking the twine a second time under the final half-hitch. Pull tight, and trim (p. 25) the ends, leaving a short end.

SAILMAKER'S WHIPPING

This whipping gives the most secure finish to the end of a length of *three-strand rope*. It has the appearance of a Palm and Needle Whipping I (p. 164), but it can be made without a needle or a *palm*. Even though it is not stitched onto the rope, if made carefully it will neither slide off the end of the rope, nor will it easily unravel. When making this whipping, take care to maintain the *lay* of the rope.

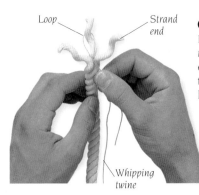

Loop

Strand end

Whipping twine

❶ Unlay (p. 23) the end of a length of rope. Form a *loop* near one end of the *whipping twine*, and pass it over one of the strand ends so that the neck of the loop lies in the center of the strand ends. Hold the loop together with a finger and thumb.

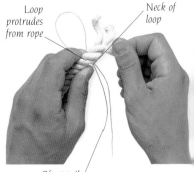

Loop protrudes from rope

Neck of loop

Short tail

❷ Relay (p. 23) the strand ends so that the neck of the loop is caught in the center of the rope, leaving a short tail.

Loop

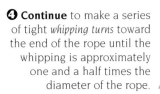

Short tail

❸ Working toward the end of the rope, wrap the whipping twine around the rope. Leave the loop and short tail free.

Whipping turns

❹ Continue to make a series of tight *whipping turns* toward the end of the rope until the whipping is approximately one and a half times the diameter of the rope.

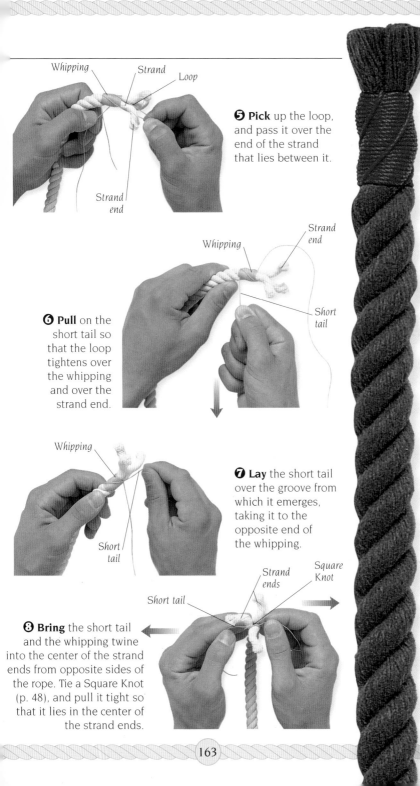

❺ Pick up the loop, and pass it over the end of the strand that lies between it.

Whipping — Strand — Loop

Strand end

Whipping — Strand end

Short tail

❻ Pull on the short tail so that the loop tightens over the whipping and over the strand end.

Whipping

Short tail

❼ Lay the short tail over the groove from which it emerges, taking it to the opposite end of the whipping.

Strand ends — Square Knot

Short tail

❽ Bring the short tail and the whipping twine into the center of the strand ends from opposite sides of the rope. Tie a Square Knot (p. 48), and pull it tight so that it lies in the center of the strand ends.

PALM & NEEDLE WHIPPING I

Favored by *riggers* and sailmakers, the Palm and Needle Whipping requires a *palm* to protect the hand, and a needle threaded with *whipping twine*. The first variation of this whipping works well on *braided rope* with a core (p. 11), since it locks the core of the rope to its outer layers. The *frapping turns* need to lie as flat as possible in order to avoid unnecessary wear.

Whipping twine

Needle

Palm

Tail

Second stitch

❶ Insert a needle toward the end of a length of braided rope. Pull the whipping twine through, leaving a short tail. Working toward the end of the rope, make one stitch on each side of the rope. Catch the short tail in the second stitch, and pull the twine tight.

❷ Working away from the end of the rope, and covering the stitches just made, wrap the whipping twine tightly around the rope to form *whipping turns*.

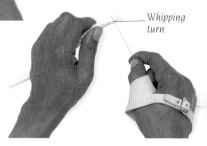

Whipping turn

Whipping

❸ When the whipping is about one and a half times the diameter of the rope, push the needle through the rope at the end of the whipping. Pull the whipping twine tightly through.

❹ Pass the whipping twine over the whipping. Insert the needle through the rope at the end of the whipping, and pull the whipping twine through. Repeat to complete a frapping turn and secure the whipping in place.

Whipping twine is pulled through

Frapping turn

Second frapping turn

❺ Repeat Step 4 to form a second frapping turn next to the first. Pull the twine tight.

Frapping turns

❻ Insert the point of the needle between the two frapping turns from front to back. Pass it under one frapping turn and pull the thread through.

❼ Pass the whipping twine over both frapping turns. Insert the needle under the second frapping turn and up between the frapping turns. Pull the twine tight.

First frapping turn *Second frapping turn*

Knot

❽ Insert the needle into the base of the knot just formed and through to the other side of the rope.

Knot lies within rope

❾ Pull the whipping twine through tightly so that the knot around the frapping turns disappears into the rope. Trim (p. 25) the whipping twine.

PALM & NEEDLE WHIPPING II

This whipping for *three-strand rope* begins and finishes in the same way as the Palm and Needle Whipping I (p. 164), with the *frapping turns* laid along the grooves of the rope.

Whipping

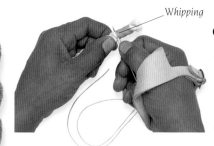

❶ Complete Steps 1–2 of the Palm and Needle Whipping I. Insert the needle into the grooves on either side of one strand at the bottom of the whipping. Pull the twine through.

❷ To make a frapping turn, lay the *whipping twine* over the line of the groove from which it emerges. Insert the needle through to the next groove, and pull the twine through.

Frapping turn

Whipping twine

Third frapping turn

❸ Lay the twine back over the whipping along the groove, and stitch through to the next groove. Repeat once more, bringing the needle out through the first groove, to make three frapping turns. Pull the whipping twine tight.

Doubled frapping turns

❹ Make a second cycle of frapping turns beside the first. Follow Steps 6–9 of the Palm and Needle Whipping I to finish the knot.

WEST COUNTRY WHIPPING

The origin of the name of this whipping is unknown. It consists of a series of Overhand Knots (p. 28), and works particularly well around the end of *large-diameter rope* and *cable*. Work back from the end of the rope so that the finished knot will not work loose.

❶ Form a loose Overhand Knot in the center of a length of *whipping twine*, tucking the left strand through the right strand. Pass the Overhand Knot over the end of a rope, and pull as tight as possible.

Overhand Knot

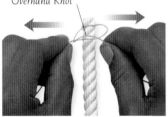

Second Overhand Knot

❷ Turn the rope over, and tie a second Overhand Knot under the first, tucking the left strand through the right strand as before. Pull tight.

❸ Continue to tie a series of Overhand Knots on alternate sides of the rope, working away from the end of the rope, until the whipping is one and a half times the diameter of the rope.

Whipping

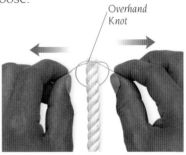

Square Knot

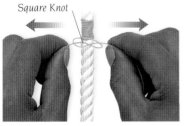

❹ To secure the whipping, tie a Square Knot (p. 48) by tucking the right rope through the left rope after the final Overhand Knot has been made. Pull tight, and trim (p. 25) the ends of the whipping twine.

SEIZING

A *seizing* binds two parts of rope side by side. The friction generated by a seizing is sufficient to hold immense loads. For centuries the heavy *standing rigging* on ships, which held the masts in place, was seized rather than knotted or spliced. It is important to tie a seizing evenly and tightly to make sure that it is secure.

Constrictor Knot

Whipping twine

❶ With the end of a length of *whipping twine*, tie a tight Constrictor Knot (p. 57) around the two parts of rope to be seized.

Turn

❷ Make a series of *turns* around the two parts of rope, tightening each one as it is made.

Seizing

Pull whipping twine through

❸ Make enough turns for a seizing three times the diameter of the rope. Begin to secure the seizing with a *frapping turn*, taking the whipping twine down between the two parts of rope.

Seizing

❹ Take the whipping twine over the seizing, then between the parts of rope at the other end of the seizing.

Frapping turn

Seizing

❺ Bring the whipping twine back over the seizing and down between the two parts of rope again. This completes one frapping turn. Pull the whipping twine tightly around the seizing.

❻ Make a second complete frapping turn so that two strands of whipping twine are pulled tightly across the seizing on both sides.

First frapping turn

Second frapping turn

Frapping turns

❼ To lock the frapping turns in place, bring the whipping twine up between the two parts of rope, then up between the frapping turns and under one of the frapping turns. Take the whipping twine over both turns, and tuck it into the center of the turns.

❽ Pull the twine tight to draw the knot down between the two lengths of rope. Trim (p. 25) the twine, leaving a short end.

Knot disappears between ropes

STITCH & SEIZE

B<i>raided rope</i> that has been doubled back on itself can be formed into a permanent <i>eye</i> by stitching the two parts of rope together and making a <i>seizing</i> over the stitches. Make sure that the seizing is pulled very tight. Use a sailmaker's needle and <i>whipping twine</i> to make the stitches, pushing the needle through the rope with a <i>palm</i> to protect the hand.

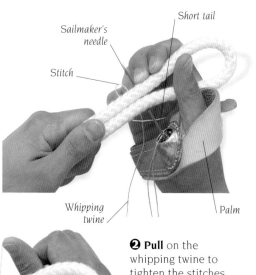

Short tail

Sailmaker's
needle

Stitch

❶ **Make** two stitches through the two parts of rope to be bound together, one on each side of the ropes. Catch the short tail of the whipping twine in the second stitch.

Whipping
twine

Palm

❷ **Pull** on the whipping twine to tighten the stitches so that the short tail lies against the rope.

Second
stitch

Short tail

❸ **Wrap** the whipping twine around the two parts of rope to make a *turn*. Follow Steps 3–8 for the Seizing (p. 168) to complete the knot.

Turn

GLOSSARY

The glossary explains the meaning of terms that occur in this book. It includes terms used to refer to rope and terms used in the instructions for tying the knots. It also explains some specialized climbing and sailing terms. Some entries refer you to the section Using Rope (pp. 8–25), where they are more fully explained.

BELAY To attach one climber to another with a rope that will absorb the shock of a fall.

BIGHT 1 A part of a rope folded back on itself to form a narrow loop (p. 20). **2** The curved side of a knot.

BLOOD KNOT A knot consisting of many turns, usually angling or climbing knots.

BOAT HOOK A pole with a hook, used to catch hold of a rope, ring, or small boat.

BODY The bulky, tied part of a knot.

BOLLARD A small post made of wood or metal on a boat or on a dock. A bollard is used for securing a mooring rope.

BRACE A length of wood or metal used to strengthen or support a structure.

BRAID Strands or yarns woven or braided together in a regular pattern.

BRAIDED ROPE Rope made by weaving or braiding strands or yarn together (p. 11).

BRAKING ROPE The part of a rope that can be used to control the amount of slip of a knot, and that will limit the amount of slip of a knot during a fall.

BREAKING LOAD The amount of load that will cause a new rope to break in test conditions. The safe working load of a rope in good condition can be calculated by reducing the test breaking load according to the circumstances in which the rope is to be used (p. 15).

CABLE A large rope made by twisting together three lengths of three-strand rope. Cable is usually S-laid (p. 10).

CHAFE A frayed part of a rope caused by the repeated rubbing of the rope against an abrasive surface.

CLEAT A wooden or metal fitting around which a rope is wound to secure it.

COIL Rope made up into a neat series of circles or loops, usually before storage.

CORDAGE A general term used for ropes of all types and sizes.

CORE The inner part of a rope made from parallel, twisted, or braided fibers (p. 11).

CROSSING TURN A circle of rope made by crossing a rope over itself (p. 20).

DECK QUOITS Circles of rope used to play a game on board ship in which the circles are thrown over a fixed peg.

ELASTICATED CORD See *shock cord*.

EYE 1 A hole in a knot. **2** The hole inside a circle of rope. **3** A permanent loop made at the end of a length of rope. **4** The opening at the end of a hook through which fishing line is threaded.

FID A pointed tool made from wood used for separating strands of rope.

FRAPPING TURNS Additional turns made across lashing, whipping, or seizing turns. Frapping turns are used to tighten the previous layer of turns.

HALF-HITCH A circle of rope made around an object. The circle is kept in place by taking one end of the rope across and at right angles to the other end.

HALYARD A rope used for the raising or lowering of sails.

HARD-LAID ROPE Three-strand rope that has been twisted very tightly in construction so that it is stiff and firm.

HEAVING LINE A light line that is attached to a mooring rope. It is thrown from a boat and used to haul a mooring rope ashore.

HOLDFAST Any fitting or fixed object to which a rope under strain can be attached to secure it in place.

KERNMANTEL The term for climbing ropes made with a twisted core (kern) and a braided sheath (mantel).

LAID ROPE Rope formed by twisting strands of yarn together (p. 10).

LARGE-DIAMETER ROPE Rope that is about $^{15}/_{16}$ inch in diameter or larger.

LASH; LASHING To secure two or more adjacent or crossed poles with a binding of rope; the term for the binding.

LASHING TURN A turn used to bind poles together as part of a lashing.

LAY The direction of the twist of the strands in laid rope (p. 10).

LEAD The number of strands used to make a braid, used especially with reference to a Turk's Head knot.

LINE A length of rope that is less than ³⁄₁₆ inch in diameter.

LOADED ROPE The part of a rope that is used to apply force to a climbing knot.

LOOP A circle of rope made by bringing two parts of rope together without crossing them over each other (p. 20).

MARLINGSPIKE A slim, pointed metal cone used to separate strands of rope, usually when untying a knot (p. 21).

NETTING NEEDLE A pointed tool for carrying a quantity of fine line when making a net (p. 21).

PALM A glovelike leather strap fitted with a metal plate (iron). It is worn on the hand to protect the palm when pushing a sailmaker's needle through rope (p. 21).

PULLEY BLOCK Grooved wheels set in a frame, used to gain purchase on rope or to change the direction of its course.

RIGGER A person who specializes in the making of rigging for yachts and ships.

RIGGING The arrangement of ropes and spars that control the sails of a ship.

ROUND TURN A complete circle followed by a half circle made with a rope around an object (p. 21).

RUNNING RIGGING Mobile rigging that controls the sails and spars of a ship.

S-LAID ROPE Laid rope with twists following the center line of the letter S (p. 10).

SCREWGATE CARABINER An oval or D-shaped metal snaplink with a screw-locking device, used by climbers.

SEIZE; SEIZING To join two ropes or two parts of a rope by binding them with twine; the term used for the binding.

SHEATH A covering of woven strands protecting a core of rope (p. 11).

SHEET A rope that controls a sail.

SHOCK CORD Rope with a very high degree of stretch. It consists of a rubber elastic core protected by a braided sheath usually made from nylon fibers. Shock cord is also known as elasticated cord.

SHORTENING A knot used to shorten a long length of rope temporarily.

SLING A continuous circle of rope or tape. A sling can be made by tying the ends of the rope or tape with a Fisherman's Knot (p. 74) or a Water (Tape) Knot (p. 77). A sling is also known as a strop.

SMALL-DIAMETER ROPE Rope that is about ³⁄₁₆–⁵⁄₁₆ inch in diameter.

SMALL STUFF A general, imprecise term for small-diameter rope or line.

SPADE END The flattened end of a hook that has no eye.

SPAR The term for a wooden or metal pole used on a ship.

STANDING PART The reserve amount of rope not immediately active during the tying of a knot (p. 20).

STANDING RIGGING Rigging that is fixed in position on a ship.

STROP See sling.

SWEDISH FID A tool with a hollow, pointed metal blade, used for tucking strand ends when splicing stiff rope.

TAPE Flat woven webbing used by climbers to make slings.

THIN LINE A length of line that is less than ¹⁄₁₆ inch in diameter.

THREE-STRAND ROPE Rope made of three strands twisted together (p. 10).

TUCK The passing of one part of a rope underneath another part.

TURN The passing of a rope around one side of an object (p. 21).

UNLAID ROPE Rope that has been separated into its component strands.

WHIPPING TURN A turn made around the end of a rope as part of a whipping.

WHIPPING TWINE Thin line, often made of nylon, used to bind the end of a rope.

WORKING END The end of a rope used during the tying of a knot (p. 20).

WORKING LOAD The maximum load that should be put on a rope while it is in use.

YARN Natural or synthetic fibers that have been twisted into threads.

Z-LAID ROPE Laid rope with twists following the center line of the letter Z (p. 10).

INDEX

ACKNOWLEDGMENTS

AUTHOR'S ACKNOWLEDGMENTS

I would like to thank all those users of knots down the centuries who have passed on their knowledge so that I can be in a position to do the same today. I am also grateful to the members of the International Guild of Knot Tyers, who have been an inspiration to me and have given me much support. If you wish to share their joy in knots, contact the Guild at the address given below. I also owe thanks to Peter Collingwood for freely allowing me to show his recently discovered Boa Knot, and John Smith for the Icicle Hitch. I would like to thank Adèle Hayward, Darren Hill, and the rest of the team at Dorling Kindersley for helping me to make this book. Finally, special thanks to my wife, Liz, who, as always, has supported and encouraged me in this project, and also to Jenny Bennet, who first showed me that I could write.

PUBLISHER'S ACKNOWLEDGMENTS

Original edition produced by: **Project editor** Adèle Hayward, **Designer** Darren Hill, **Editor** Julie Oughton, **Assistant Designer** Simon Oon, **Production Controller** Alison Jones, **DTP Designer** Jason Little, **Managing Editor** Stephanie Jackson, **Managing Art Editor** Nigel Duffield.

DK Publishing, Inc. would like to thank the following:

Consultants George Steele and Joseph P. Schmidbauer.

Editorial and Design Assistance Alison Coles for editorial assistance; Josephine Bryan and Catherine Rubinstein for testing and proofreading; Chris Bernstein for the index; Sasha Kennedy, Rachel Symons, and Laura Watson for design assistance.

Illustrations Darren Hill.

Photography Andy Crawford, Steve Gorton, Gary Ombler.

Hand Modeling Molly Anderson, Steve Benjamin, Sara Freeman, David Groves, Toby Heran, Chris Hill, Darren Hill, Pepukai Makoni, Ingrid Wakeling, Howard Watson.

INTERNATIONAL GUILD OF KNOT TYERS

Founded in England in 1982, the IGKT is a registered charity with members all over the world. It aims to promote the art, craft, and science of knotting, and its membership is open to all who are interested in knots. Details are available from the following addresses:

IGKT–NAB
John Burke – Secretary
4417 Academy
Dearborn Heights, MI 48125–2205

IGKT–PAB
Joseph Schmidbauer – Secretary
1805 Kingsford Dr.
Corona, CA 91720

IGKT–Texas Branch
Gary Sessions – Secretary
2841 Gladiolus Lane
Dallas, TX 75233

www.igkt.net

Please note: The scope of this book allows us to explain some, but not all, the potential hazards and risks of knot tying. Whilst it has been prepared with the safety of your person and property in mind, you can reduce the risk to yourself and to your property by adopting a careful, cautious approach. If you intend to use any knot in a potentially hazardous or life-threatening situation, always seek specialist advice from a qualified professional.